Shooting Star

Shooting

Star

THE RISE & FALL OF THE
BRITISH MOTORCYCLE INDUSTRY

Abe Aamidor

ECW Press

Published by ECW Press, 2120 Queen Street East, Suite 200,
Toronto, Ontario, Canada M4E 1E2 / 416.694.3348 / info@ecwpress.com

LIBRARY AND ARCHIVES CANADA CATALOGUING IN PUBLICATION

Aamidor, Abraham
Shooting star : the rise & fall of the British motorcycle industry / Abe Aamidor.

ISBN 978-1-55022-900-4

1. Motorcycle industry — Great Britain — History.
2. Motorcycles — Great Britain — History. I. Title.

HD9710.5.G72A24 2009   338.4'762922750941   C2009-902518-3

Design: Tania Craan
Cover images © John Dean, used by permission of Reynolds-Alberta Museum
Typesetting: Mary Bowness
Printing: Friesens   1   2   3   4   5

Printed on paper with 100% recycled content.

PRINTED AND BOUND IN CANADA

ECW PRESS
ecwpress.com

Contents

Acknowledgements

I never appreciated the acknowledgements page in a book until I published my first book. Acknowledgements deservedly go to people who read manuscripts for clarity, thoroughness, and accuracy as well as to people who agree to be interviewed at length or who provide good tips and sources for further research. Typically, acknowledgements go to people who help to bring a project to a successful completion and who do so without any self-interest.

Almost everyone cited in this book whom I was able to contact personally deserves an acknowledgement. I was continually amazed how almost no one whom I contacted gave me the cold shoulder. Virtually everyone took me at my word that I was writing a serious book about the rise and fall of the British motorcycle industry, and they all went above and beyond the call of duty to help me, even enthusiastically so in many cases.

I cannot mention all of those deserving thanks here — all help was valuable — but some contributors stand out. Jeff Smith, who was with me on this project almost from the beginning, provided information, tips, and photos and reviewed the manuscript for accuracy. Any errors that have slipped through are my responsibility alone. Michael "Old Mike" Jackson became a friend during the process of writing this book — he provided information, background, tips, sources, photos, as well as encouragement. He also reviewed the text for accuracy. Industry veteran William Colquhoun further reviewed the text for me.

The Motorcycle Hall of Fame and Museum in Pickerington, Ohio, and the Barber Vintage Motorsports Museum in Birmingham, Alabama, United States, both provided me with useful archival material. Norman Vanhouse, Don Rickman, Don Brown, Bobby Hill, and a host of other notables from both sides of the Atlantic in the 1940s–60s were also wonderful to interview. I read many books on the subject — Barry Ryerson's earlier study of BSA and Jeff Clew's biography of industry giant Edward Turner stand out.

Indirectly, at least, I have to acknowledge both the executives and the shop floor workers in the British motorcycle industry. If they hadn't created their own history, there would have been nothing for me to write about.

Finally, and at the risk of sounding gratuitous, I must acknowledge the role of publisher Jack David in bringing this book to the light of day. This is my fourth book, but increasingly book publishing is becoming an insider's game, or you have to conform to some business model, meaning you're just churning out product, not actually creating anything. Independent, free-thinking publishers are hugely important to democracy, to free speech and intelligent discourse on a wide range of subjects. I did not know Mr. David before contacting him, but we established a clear and honest exchange that led to a publishing deal. I didn't have to knock down 20 doors first or have a high-powered New York agent.

Introduction

If, as the saying goes, Britannia ruled the waves, it's just as true that it ruled the motorcycle lanes of the world. Today there are famous brands such as Honda in Japan, Harley-Davidson in America, and BMW in Germany. Yet any number of British marques belong in a motorcycle hall of fame. Velocette was founded by German immigrants circa 1905 and based in Birmingham. The family-owned business produced overhead-cam engines in the 1920s and introduced the positive-stop, foot-operated transmission, a feature eventually adopted by every other motorcycle manufacturer in the world. Norton, organized in 1898, built the most successful Grand Prix racer in motorcycle history — the lusty Manx Norton — and also made the Commando, the last great British "superbike" of the 1970s. Norton, too, was based in Birmingham for most of the brand's life.

Triumph traces its roots to German-Jewish immigrant Siegfried Bettmann and produced its first motorcycle under the Triumph name in 1902. Its great innovation was a successful range of "parallel twin" motorcycle engines dating from 1937; this design became the standard for both the British and the Japanese industries for the next 30 years. It is a twin-cylinder Triumph Thunderbird that Marlon Brando rides in the 1953 Hollywood release *The Wild One*.

Other important manufacturers included AJS, Matchless, Brough Superior (very limited production, but it's the brand T.E. Lawrence rode when he crashed and died in 1935), Royal Enfield (still produced under that name in India but not England), Douglas, Greeves, Vincent, James, Ariel, Scott, New Imperial, and others.

The biggest motorcycle manufacturer of all was BSA. The company was incorporated in 1861 by a consortium of Birmingham rifle manufacturers that had supplied the British army during the Crimean War. To the firm's very end, in 1973, its symbolism included a "piled arms" motif. For a time, BSA claimed that it was "the most popular motorcycle in the world" or that "one in four is a BSA," and it was true. As proof of BSA's importance, the British government convinced Lord Shawcross, the former Labour Party MP and esteemed chief prosecutor at the 1946 Nuremberg war crimes tribunal, to become chairman of BSA Group in 1971, when it was in its deepest financial crisis.

Overall, the British motorcycle industry was the third largest source of foreign exchange in the United Kingdom in the years immediately following World War II, after motorcars and Scotch whisky. Yet by 1974, the British brands held only 1 percent of the all-important American market and just 3 percent of their home market.[1]

Motorcycles were as important to England's national identity as the wine industry is to France's national identity to this day or horse breeding is to Kentucky's identity. The first purpose-built, fully banked automobile and motorcycle racetrack in the world was built at Brooklands, near London, in 1907, two years before the Indianapolis Motor Speedway opened. Also in 1907, the most famous motorcycle race in the world, the TT (short for Tourist Trophy), began at the nearby Isle of Man. The prestigious International Six Days Trial, an event still in existence, began in England in 1913, and the most feared motocross course in the world in the 1950s and '60s was at Hawkstone Park in Shropshire, complete with a monster hill as long and as steep as a roller-coaster ride.

Just as in any sport, business, or military hierarchy, the world of motorcycling had its panoply of important players. Several stand out. Geoff Duke, a motorcycle dispatch rider during World War II, was the last Briton to win a road-racing world championship on a British motorcycle — he did this on a Manx Norton in 1952. He was a hero off the track, too, by publicly supporting a riders' strike by underpaid privateers at the 1955 Dutch Grand Prix. Jeff Smith, a former apprentice at BSA in the early 1950s, was the last British rider to win a world motocross championship on a British bike — he did this in 1964 and 1965 on a BSA Victor that he had helped to develop.

Important engineers and tuners included Norton's Joe Craig. This former racer's remuneration was linked to the firm's track successes, so much so that once he became chief engineer at Norton he largely ignored development of production models in favour of his racing machines. Other prominent engineers were BSA's Roland Pike, whose unpublished memoirs have only recently been discovered, and the tall, eccentric Francis Beart, a private tuner who once designed a race car for Cooper that used a motorcycle engine and chain drive to the rear axle. Polish émigré Leo Kuzmicki, a former university lecturer in Warsaw and a volunteer Royal Air Force pilot in England during World War II, became a leading development engineer at Norton and later for Chrysler, the car manufacturer. Soichiro Honda, the least stereotypical of all Japanese industrial leaders, is profiled. American styling guru Craig Vetter, who created the radical Triumph X-75 Hurricane introduced in 1973, is also featured.

Perhaps the most interesting men in the industry, albeit least well known to the public, were the businessmen behind the scenes. London-born Edward Turner, rather middlebrow by upbringing but very imperious in his management style, served a stint in the merchant navy in World War I and worked at odd jobs before opening a motorcycle repair shop in the early 1920s. Turner later designed motorcycles that were technologically advanced for their day and beautifully styled; he is best associated with the Triumph brand. Bert Hopwood was an influential designer and manager at all three of the most important British marques — BSA, Norton, and Triumph.

The godfather of the industry was Jack Sangster, who worked backroom deals to buy the Ariel and Triumph motorcycle lines early in his career, then wrested control of industry giant BSA in one of the most well-publicized boardroom rebellions in British history in 1956. Dennis Poore ended up as the most hated man in England by the 1970s because the British motorcycle industry died on his watch, yet it was he who saved Norton in the late 1960s and almost saved Triumph in the 1970s.

Other deserving men of motorcycling are profiled here, such as world champion road racers John Surtees and Mike Hailwood, both of whom started their racing careers on British machinery but won their world championships on Italian and Japanese bikes. Don and Derek Rickman designed, built, and marketed their own motocross racing chassis that was better than anything the major British manufacturers developed, so much so that all the companies refused to sell the brothers engines. There's also colourful Swedish rider Bill Nilsson, the self-described dirtiest rider in the 1950s. The ineffable Bill Johnson, a well-to-do San Francisco lawyer who became Triumph's most important distributor in America, is profiled too. Alf Child, a British ex-patriate who helped to sell Harley-Davidson motorcycles in sub-Sahara Africa and in imperial Japan, all prior to World War II, is introduced. They are the supporting cast, as it were, in a freewheeling, barnstorming era gone by.

Most dramatically, the 1973–75 Triumph motorcycle factory sit-in at Meriden — one of the longest, most destructive, and best publicized industrial actions in all of British history — is chronicled for the first time in convincing detail here. Anthony Wedgwood "Tony" Benn, the noted Labour Party leader, wanted to nationalize much of British industry, and he used the motorcycle crisis of the early 1970s as a test case. Proof of this secret plan was made public only in 2005, after a "30-year" rule on confidential government documents expired.

To this day, machines such as the BSA Gold Star, Triumph Bonneville, Velocette Thruxton, Vincent Black Shadow, Norton Commando, and a few others continue to be the most sought after collectible motorcycles in the world. The question has to be asked: if the motorcycles were so appealing, why did their man- ufacturers go out of business? The visual appeal of the machinery is legendary: "The Art of the Motorcycle," a 1998 exhibit at New York's Guggenheim Museum that promoted dozens of European and American motorcycle designs as rolling sculpture, proved to be the most popular exhibit at the museum up to that time. The prettiest motorcycles on display, often with shades of eggshell blue and deep reds with chromium highlights and taste- ful gold pin striping, were the British machines.

Other books have highlighted one or another marque or pro- filed this or that famous rider. But this book is a full dramatic narrative, the first synthesis that ties together all the influences on the British motorcycle industry, from the design, manufac- ture, and marketing of the bikes and the impact of Honda beginning in 1959 to the men who both produced the bikes and rode them. This history also reviews for the first time virtually all of the professional economic and business analyses made of the industry, but it does so in layman's terms. There are lessons to be learned here as the North American automobile companies con- tinue to face brutal challenges from the Japanese, Korean, and high-end German manufacturers.

A gallery of full-colour, exhibit-quality photos is reproduced by permission of the Reynolds-Alberta Museum in Canada, which staged its own major motorcycle retrospective in 2005 and 2006. Each featured photo comes with a synopsis of why the machine is important. Plenty of historical black-and-white photos are included throughout the text too.

This book investigates claims that the British motorcycle industry's fall was due in part to its penchant for holding on to old designs, old machine tools, and old factories (e.g., an unwill- ingness to plough profits into research and development and new technology) as well as an utter disregard for market share eco- nomics. The Japanese took a different tack — they were willing to sustain losses if they would lead to increased market share, and they were adroit at creating new demand, not merely steal- ing sales from the Americans or British. Some British factories were dark, cramped, and inefficient — parts and subassemblies often were moved about on wheeled carts, and skilled craftsmen often would bolt everything together by hand. Testing of proto-types often was informal — some bloke would be told to ride an early production model home, or just down to London and back, and report back what he thought.

An independent study ordered by Parliament in 1975 con-cluded that the British motorcycle industry ultimately sought to survive by abandoning one market segment after another in which it could not compete, until it could compete in none. The researchers also found that Japanese workers weren't paid less than their British counterparts. The Japanese manufacturing techniques simply were more capital intensive, which meant vastly increased productivity and better quality.

The charge that the British did not invest in new technology and new machines is not always accurate, though. Various man-ufacturers did invest in new products, but they were the wrong products. Virtually every significant British motorcycle manufac-turer developed a line of motor scooters in the late 1950s or early 1960s, but they all failed miserably in the marketplace. BMW and Harley-Davidson did not invest heavily in scooters, and those brands are still with us. The largest British manufacturer, BSA Group, also spent lavishly on a new design and research centre at Umberslade Hall in the late 1960s, but there were few positive returns. The failure there was poor engineering. British motorcy-cle producers in 1962 also complained about a disastrous Anglo-Japanese free-trade agreement that year that exempted small motorcycles from any import restrictions in England but did nothing to help British exports to Japan. Every postmortem on the industry since said they were right to howl.

It's clear the industry also suffered the usual problems with labour. "If you wanted to introduce a new machine, you could not introduce it without a renegotiation of the piece work rate which might take months," said veteran motorcycle journalist Frank Melling. "If you wanted to modify the overhead track, you couldn't do that. You had to negotiate that."

BSA factory employees were prompted to "down tools and walk out on strike" after a commercial photographer dared to plug in his own lights for a catalogue shoot of new models in the late 1950s — only a union electrician was allowed to do that."[II] And, when Norton Villiers Triumph (NVT) owner Dennis Poore wanted to shut down Triumph motorcycle manufacture at Meriden in the dark days of 1973 and shift production to the BSA factory in Small Heath, which NVT also owned by then, the Triumph workers locked management out for 18 months. It was one of the last spasms of the industry.

Yet most British motorcycle industry workers were much more competent than outsiders understood. In Birmingham, Coventry, Wolverhampton, London, and Meriden, sons worked alongside their fathers, and management control over the shop floor often was delegated to experienced craft workers. It was said that many small labour disputes could be resolved in a break room over a packet of Woodbine cigarettes — that is, informally and collegially. A London *Times* reporter once asked Meriden workers how long they had been there. He said people would tell him "'I'm a newcomer, I've only been here eight, nine, ten years.' Most told me twenty, thirty or even forty."[III]

These were men who viewed themselves truly as craftsmen and not merely low-skilled production workers who only had to perform simple tasks all day, which in part is how the Japanese and eventually European manufacturers viewed their production line employees. The British almost handmade their motorcycles in what were often glorified workshops while the rest of the world continued to improve on Henry Ford's assembly line model.

Many survivors of the industry were interviewed in person, by phone, or via e-mail for this book. Anyone quoted by name actually spoke the words to me or was quoted word for word by a reliable secondary source, which is properly cited. I had a stroke of good fortune in obtaining a lengthy, ultra-rare interview with Edward Turner from a source in England that was recorded shortly before his death — I could actually hear the man speak. I collected many out-of-print books on the industry and obtained an official, rare BSA film that included a full tour of the giant factory in Small Heath, a Birmingham suburb. In cases where multiple sources provide the same, essentially uncontested information, I treat it all as fact, without crediting one or another source for the information. I have tried to add colour where appropriate — the broad grin or the sly smile, the highly polished alloy engine cases, the dangerously off-camber corner on a slippery racetrack, or the long aprons worn by technicians on the shop floor inside those dark factories — but I'm not writing poetry. The goal of this book is good storytelling, authentic history, and just bringing things alive as much as possible.

Although this book includes the claim that the British motorcycle industry has ended, a new Triumph Motorcycle Company was established by John Bloor and began producing a full range of motorcycles in Hinckley, England, in 1991. Bloor, a real estate developer and self-made millionaire, bought the old Triumph factory and name in 1983, then built a new, modern, largely automated factory over the next several years. The company is successful, producing a line of modern, liquid-cooled, multi-cylinder bikes as well as retro-looking, air-cooled twins, so perhaps I should say the British motorcycle industry has been resurrected. But the old, regal industry — with rorty engines and metal fenders and gas tanks delicately stamped and painted in small shops by craftsmen who could have built the entire bikes by themselves if they were asked to — has in fact ended.

Chapter One

Patriarchs

Y OUNG FRANK MELLING, then a weekend racer and part-
time correspondent for several motorcycle magazines in
England and America, was the most hated man in Birmingham in 1971. He had recently written that young riders in the
all-important American market, who were more loyal to legendary marques BSA, Triumph, and Norton than those who flew
the Union Jack itself, were in open revolt over quality issues with
the rorty, road-burning 650 cc and 750 cc machines for which
the British were so famous. Melling wrote that the Americans
were upset because multi-cylinder "superbikes" from Honda and
Kawasaki were now better, faster, and cheaper than anything the
British offered.

Melling wrote that the Americans were right to be angry, and
he laid the blame at the seat of power inside the BSA Group at
Small Heath, Birmingham, England. Until recently, BSA Group
had been one of the largest companies in the United Kingdom,

with 67 subsidiaries, including luxury Daimler cars, industrial machine tools, a variety of armaments, and the iconic London taxis, plus several motorcycle lines.

After a particularly vile column, the main publicist for BSA Group, Reg Dancer, rang Melling on the phone, inviting him up to the executive suite inside company headquarters at Small Heath to see the managing director himself, Lionel Jofeh (pronounced joe-fee).

"He said, 'Would you prefer I call you Frank, or should I call you Melling?' This was very much university stuff," Melling recalled. "He was going on, 'Yes, we can see you're right, and I see you're upset. Would you like to come down and speak to Jofeh?' So I went down to the Birmingham train station, and I get off there, and they send a taxi, BSA 1, and standing there is a guy with a card with my name. 'Melling, would you please come this way.' BSA 1 had its own parking space. We get to the factory, and I'm in my only white shirt and my only jacket without holes in it. The press agent says, 'If you wouldn't mind, would you come this way?' We go up the steps and go up to this magnificent boardroom, and we had sherry in silver glasses."

Melling was a flower child in those days every bit as much as he was a motorcycle enthusiast. Around his neck he wore a flower-patterned tie, and his silky polyester shirt was topped by a jacket with puffed shoulders and wide, pointy lapels. On his feet he wore soft, ankle-high suede shoes, like pixies wore. Everyone else in the room was in a dark wool Savile Row suit or equivalent. The boardroom itself had a large teak table in the middle and a wall lined with bookcases with glass doors; Melling noted that many of the books were export manuals.

"Jofeh looked at me the way George Bush would look at a Taliban fighter," Melling said. "But he had been briefed to be nice to me. I was like a baby being set up to have his tummy tickled. Then Jofeh said, 'The thing is, you're looking at motorcycles the wrong way. You're looking at them as motorcycles. We're looking at them as units of production, as consumer durables.' I stood up above Jofeh and said that's wrong. He said, 'You know nothing about motorcycles.' And I said, 'You know nothing about your customers.' He said, 'Who are you to tell me I know nothing about my customers.' I said, 'I'm one of your customers.'"

The year was 1971. Within two months Lionel Jofeh would be out of a job, and within two years BSA would be out of existence. And soon after that workers at the former Triumph subsidiary in nearby Meriden would start one of the longest sit-ins in British industrial history. Soon the for sale signs would be up on old brick British motorcycle factories everywhere.

The British ruled from London, but they got things done in Birmingham. The gritty West Midlands capital, home to the industrial revolution as much as Athens was the birthplace of Western civilization, was where motorcars and BSA Gold Stars and Spitfire fighter planes were made, where long trains brought in the coal from Wales and flat-bottom boats carried cargo in and out of the city on its famous man-made canals. Generations of staunch workers with felt caps on their heads and tin lunch pails under their arms filed in to work every day to actually do the jobs.

Home to the bicycle boom in the late Victorian era, Birmingham hosted many of the leading motorcycle manufacturers in the twentieth century. Norton, the most famous road-racing brand in the world at one time, the Ferrari of its domain, was founded in 1898 by Birmingham native James Norton, the son of a cabinet maker. The Norton Manufacturing Company initially produced chains and other bicycle parts, then began assembling complete motorcycles using parts from other manufacturers as early as 1902. Its most famous models included the Manx Norton, a 500 cc single-cylinder model that won many important road races worldwide over a 30-year span, and the Commando, the last of the British superbikes in the 1970s.

Velocette, based nearby in the Hall Green suburb, was the most exclusive British motorcycle manufacturer, doing almost nothing quite like any of the other companies. The family-owned business traced its roots to German immigrant Johannes Gutgemann, who arrived in England in 1876 at age 19. Velocette pioneered the quick "positive stop" foot shift transmission, a design still in use by all motorcycle manufacturers to this day.

Ariel was a manufacturer that introduced the Rover Safety Bicycle (two similar-sized wheels, chain drive to the rear) in 1885; almost all bicycles since have had the same basic design. The firm was swallowed up by Components in 1902, a conglomerate owned by Charles Sangster and his son, Jack. Two models stand out in Ariel's history — a lithe, fast, overhead valve, single-cylinder bike, the beautifully named Red Hunter that was sold from the early 1930s to the late 1950s, and the Square Four, an unusual four-cylinder design that also had a long production run.

BSA was to become the largest motorcycle manufacturer in the city, country, and world. Incorporated in 1861, the company was founded by 14 local gunsmiths who had banded together to bid on government contracts for long rifles during the Crimean War. Each could make complete weapons in his own workshop, with hand-rubbed gunstocks and small forges and files to fashion the metal parts, but none had the space or capital to build a proper factory. They formed a "co-operative" and named the back street in the Birmingham suburb of Small Heath where most worked "Armoury Road." The name BSA itself stands for Birmingham Small Arms.

Triumph, in nearby Coventry, first introduced a motorcycle in 1902 using a small Belgian-made motor. The company's German-Jewish founder, Siegfried Bettmann, was so well liked he was elected mayor of Coventry in 1912 yet was forced to give up his post at the start of World War I because of his German heritage.[1] Triumph was to become famous for that most British of motorcycle engines, the parallel twin.

Motorcycle production thrived in Birmingham and the West Midlands throughout the 1920s and survived even into the '30s, though the Depression cut deep. Industry wide, British motorcycle production peaked at 147,000 machines in 1928, but that number plummeted to 74,400 in 1930.[2] This led to consolidation within the industry, beginning with Jack Sangster. Tall, fit, with a steady gaze and thoughtful pout underlying his aquiline nose, Sangster outwitted his board of directors and even his father, Charles, when he purchased the Ariel motorcycle division from Components in 1932. Next he fired all the employees and hired back only those he wanted, after which he moved the presses, lathes, and machine tools to suburban Selly Oak in Birmingham.

The younger Sangster, born in 1896, studied engineering at Hurstpierpont College in Sussex, in the rather more bucolic southeast part of England, then worked for a Triumph motorcycle subsidiary in Nuremberg, Germany. He got to fight the Germans during World War I as a member of the Royal Warwickshire Regiment's City of Birmingham Battalion. After demobilization, he helped to design an "opposed twin" aircooled motor for the popular Rover 8 car — it was inspired by early radial engines in use in the aircraft industry at the time and was not unlike a BMW motorcycle engine still in use. Jack joined his dad at Components in 1923, where he helped to design a car for Ariel. This was rather less successful — "the crankshaft broke like carrots,"[3] recalled one influential observer, and the failure led both father and son to concentrate on motorcycles in the future.

Ariel (the name was drawn from Shakespeare, who used it in *The Tempest* to describe an airy spirit) was almost an incubator for the British motorcycle industry in the 1920s as its personnel list was to become a who's who of the later, grander industry. Chief engineer Val Page was brought aboard from engine builder JAP in 1925 (JAP built the engine in the Brough Superior luxury motorcycle that Lawrence of Arabia crashed in 1935). It was Page who designed the single-cylinder, overhead valve engine for the company's Red Hunter model, then designed the avant-garde Ariel Leader 30 years later, the brand's last great model.

Birmingham native Bert Hopwood was an even better hire. A classically square-jawed man with bushy eyebrows and slick, dark hair, not unlike a young Sean Connery, Hopwood was a serious engineer who left school at age 14 to work in a malleable iron foundry doing all the "filthy jobs," as he put it, before taking evening classes at Birmingham Technical College. He was personally recruited to Ariel by the unselfish Page at age 18 as a junior draftsman; his first assignment was a relatively mundane task, redesigning coil valve springs for a pre-existing engine design.

Hopwood once wrote that he fell in love with motorcycles after peering through the large, plate glass windows of the Motor Cycle Emporium on swank Bristol Street in his hometown, which featured more than 100 models on display. "Motor car showrooms did not attract me," he wrote. "After all, motor car body shapes seemed to be very much alike and I felt their engines all seemed to be very similar water-cooled chunks of metal so that it was of little consequence that they were out of sight. Not so the engines of the gleaming two-wheelers, with every detail there to see. No draping of sheet metal over these beautifully finned air-cooled masterpieces."[4]

But Sangster's best hire was Edward Turner. Red-headed and round-faced, short enough to be defensive about it and imperious enough to be a snot, Turner was born into a middle-class London family in 1901 (his father, William, was a mechanical engineer). Yet he ran away and joined the merchant navy during World War 1, training to be an apprentice wireless operator. Many hundreds of British and Allied merchant vessels were sunk during that war, but the young Turner apparently was unperturbed. He complained only about the food on board — bully beef and dry biscuits that had to be banged against a hard surface to dislodge the weevils. Upon demobilization, Turner eschewed a university education, instead attending night technical school while working stints as a fitter, turner, boilermaker, and blacksmith. He also informally studied art, which was to put him miles ahead of the competition in the styling department during his long career in the motorcycle industry.[5]

In time, Turner purchased a small repair shop, Chepstow Motors, on Peckham Road in London in 1923. It was a decently sized corner shop, with large display windows on either side facing the traffic outside, a showroom on the first floor featuring a Velocette motorcycle franchise, and a grimy workshop behind the counter with rickety steps leading to a private studio on the second floor. The ruddy-faced Turner patiently performed small repairs on bicycles and old motorcycles during the day, and in the evenings he retired to the second floor, where, working long nights, apparently bereft of friends, family, or female companionship, he turned himself into a young Orville or Wilbur Wright, first designing a motorcycle from scratch, then actually building it, using many of the mechanical and metal-working skills he had learned in recent years.

Turner machined many of the parts himself on a small lathe, and in time he built an overhead cam, single-cylinder, 350 cc motorcycle engine. Later he joined together sections of steel pipe to fashion a complete frame, not unlike a bicycle's albeit with off-the-shelf spring front suspension and wheels, and dubbed his creation the Turner Special. A national motorcycle magazine soon featured engineering drawings of the design and a little blurb about the upstart young man who had built it, portraying him a bit like an English Don Quixote who would tilt at industry giants such as BSA or Triumph or Ariel.

Part showman, part workhorse, and part genius, Turner had a functioning prototype of his Special ready by 1927 that he entered in several endurance races, winning none. Then with overflowing confidence he donned one of his tight-fitting, double-breasted coats, which were to become a signature piece in his personal style, and boarded a train bound for Birmingham, where he introduced himself to executives at industry leader Ariel. Sangster and Page had read about the young man, and they respected ambition, but they didn't want the Turner Special — overhead cam motors were still considered fragile things and costly to produce, not worth the effort unless one wanted to race. Yet they were intrigued by another design the young man had imagined — a "square" four-cylinder model that existed only on a piece of paper Turner pulled from his coat pocket at the end of his interview almost as an afterthought. Single-cylinder motorcycle engines were the most popular design at the time. With relatively few parts and good cooling, they were generally reliable. Some manufacturers made V-twin motors — they could provide increased overall capacity and more horsepower but at increased cost and complexity. A few companies, particularly in America, built four-cylinder machines. They were even more complex, costly, and heavy. Plus, when mounted in line with the frame, front to back, as was always the case, they increased the motorcycle's wheelbase excessively, which adversely affected handling. But Turner's square four was different, with two upright cylinders in front and two in back, their crankshafts geared to each other. Think of a four-pack of wine — the bottles may be round, like pistons and cylinders, but the container is square. Turner's engine was not much wider than a single and was much shorter than an in-line four. Turner was hired on at Ariel in 1928.

The motorcycle was considered a logical step up from the bicycle in the early part of the twentieth century. Motorcycles were desirable because of their fuel efficiency, and most manufacturers offered sidecar options (also known as combinations) so the family could go along for a ride too. Yet the Great Depression really challenged the industry. Just as Components was forced to dispose of its Ariel motorcycle line in 1932, so too Triumph was forced into realignment the same year. The Coventry firm, which also produced cars, first sold off its bicycle line, then decided to abandon its motorcycle division in 1936.

"Would it interest you to buy Triumph?" Turner, by then chief engineer at Ariel, asked Sangster one day.

> They're not going broke, but they're going to stop making motorcycles. I said, "Jack, well, if you're not going to buy Triumph, I'm going to move on." So he went over there and negotiated with Colonel (Claude Vivian) Holbrook, who said, "We're not going to sell it. We don't want anything further to do with motorbikes. Now we want the name Triumph on our cars." Jack came back and reported to me and said it's out. I said it couldn't be out. It's an asset. You can't throw an asset away. Shareholders won't allow you to. You're prepared to offer something for it. He saw I was determined, so finally he bought the thing for nothing, practically nothing. Twenty or thirty thousand [pounds]. And

then we leased the factory. We leased the plant. We didn't buy the spares but agreed to sell them on commission. In other words, the capital venture was reduced to an absolute minimum, and I found myself sitting in the chair gathering all the pieces together seeing what I was going to do. I paid my first week's wages on an overdraft. That was the beginning of the new Triumph.[6]

The motorcycle division was renamed Triumph Engineering Company, and Sangster and Turner were in business. Turner was made general manager and chief designer and offered 5 percent of net profits, plus a 4.9 percent share in the new company itself.

The new Triumph quickly scored a triumph with the introduction in 1937 of Turner's "masterpiece," as he himself called it, the Speed Twin, a 500 cc motorcycle of parallel twin engine design. The bike was rated at 27 horsepower, a reasonable output even by modern standards, and was as light as most of its single-cylinder competitors. The Speed Twin had a desirably short wheelbase and was stylish, with a softly rounded teardrop gas tank and plenty of chrome. It was reasonably priced at 75 pounds sterling — a real winner, in other words.

Parallel twin engines were so called because they had two cylinders side by side in the engine block. This immediately gave the engine twice the number of valves for better breathing compared with single-cylinder engines of similar capacity, and the two smaller, lighter pistons always promised faster engine speed.

The motorcycling world was impressed once more with the London pom. The Speed Twin set a new standard in styling by introducing colours such as plum red and eggshell blue to motorbikes, along with an increased use of shiny chromium plate. As Turner's success became more firmly planted, resentment festered inside his number two man, Bert Hopwood, who had moved to Triumph from Ariel in 1936 along with his bosses. Hopwood was often called on to do the higher math required to improve the engineering of Turner's first drafts, which in fact were often technically deficient and were to get worse over the years. Turner always thought he was smarter than anyone else; Hopwood was not quite so arrogant, but he was certain he was smarter than Turner. "As an engineer, Edward Turner seemed to lack the technical knowledge which must be embraced if engineering design is anything but guesswork," Hopwood wrote. "However, he was an inventive genius and had a flair for pleasing shapes and an uncanny ability to 'smell out' what the buying public would readily accept."[7]

Turner and Hopwood often clashed. They were a contrast in almost everything except the size of their egos. With success, Turner purchased both a newer, Tudor-style home with central heating near Coventry and an ocean-going yacht. He also hired a full-time chauffeur, Frank Griffiths, who was to complain that his boss reduced him to the status of personal assistant, routinely browbeating him and having him prepare meals for the family on the yacht.[8]

Hopwood was less showy, often sequestering himself behind closed doors in a corner office to dream up his designs, and he maintained a home office complete with a drafting table, where he'd often work late into the night. "[Hopwood] was a very direct and very honest person," recalled long-time British motorcycle racer Jeff Smith. "He called a spade a spade in a Birmingham accent. I think that was one of his problems in the boardroom. If you spoke with a certain accent, people assumed you didn't have much of an education, which was not true."

By the late 1930s, Turner was in full flower and took an active role in marketing his products, especially in North America. In 1937, he began a correspondence with a young San Francisco lawyer who had just purchased one of Turner's 600 cc square four Ariels, resplendent with red and chrome gas tank, fishtail mufflers, and wide finning on its fat motor. Bill Johnson, a well-built, jovial man with thick, wavy hair, was born in 1905 into a wealthy Nevada banking family. Although he could have coasted in college, Johnson worked his way through Stanford University and the University of California at Los Angeles Law School as a milkman, hotel clerk, and grape picker in the San Joaquin Valley. He was not a motorcyclist in his youth but almost had a conversion experience while on his honeymoon in

Hawaii in 1936, when he took his first ride on a primitive motor scooter. Upon his return to California, the young attorney and budding entrepreneur spotted the Ariel in a motorcycle magazine, ordered one from England, and wrote to Turner asking about its design. Turner read the letter and personally replied.

In 1938, Johnson and his accountant, Wilbur Cedar, bought British and American Motors (later Johnson Motors) in Pasadena. "One Sunday I was cleaning up the place, dressed in overalls and alone," Johnson said in an interview years later. "Two men whom I immediately recognized as prominent in motorcycle circles walked in. I sensed they did not recognize me, so I went about my job, but couldn't help hearing their conversation. The gist of it was that this chap Johnson 'will never make a success of this business' as it's been tried before without success. I gathered that I had the reputation of being most affluent and somewhat of a playboy, and this motorcycle adventure was something of a hobby."[9]

Johnson was just the sort of distributor Turner was looking for — enthusiastic, hard working, and well-to-do. Although Turner had not yet been to America, he knew that was where the growth would be. Based solely on his long-distance correspondence with Turner, Johnson was awarded the West Coast distribution rights for Ariel and Triumph beginning in late 1938. The war interrupted further development of the franchise, but the partnership between Johnson and Triumph was to prove essential to the firm's postwar success.

Ironically, even though World War II interrupted commercial and enthusiast sales for all British motorcycle manufacturers, it was the conflict itself that kept the factories humming when new retail sales all but dried up. Several firms, among them BSA, Norton, Velocette, Ariel, Enfield, and James — combined to make nearly 400,000 bikes for the war effort. These most often were of classic single-cylinder design of 350 cc or 500 cc capacity. Then there was the Excelsior Welbike, a kind of folding contraption with two wheels and a motor that was used by airborne troops and often dropped into battle zones. Some of the heaviest machines, such as the Norton Big 4, a slow but reliable

600 cc bike, could handle a sidecar and carry three troops into battle, plus a mounted machine gun. The U.S. brand, Harley-Davidson, also did well during the war, selling about 80,000 machines to Allied forces.[10]

BSA shops also produced half of the precision weapons made in all of Britain, including Browning aircraft machine guns, Sten guns, Lee Enfield Short Mark III rifles, and 20 mm Oerlikon cannon.[11] BSA's managing director, James Leek, had visited a German trade fair in the mid-1930s and predicted war with the Third Reich. When war came, he was appointed by His Majesty's government to supervise armaments production in the West Midlands, including at many businesses not actually owned by BSA. He was almost a minister of state. BSA Chairman Bernard Docker also got attention from his many public acts — for example, he bought two wooden legs for a much-decorated RAF pilot who had been injured prior to the war. The gesture was widely reported in the press at the time.

There was a human cost to all this activity, of course. Birmingham's status as the industrial centre of the country made it the second most heavily bombed British city in World War II, after London itself. The bombing raids on Birmingham began on August 8, 1940, and lasted on and off until April 23, 1944. All told, nearly 9,000 people were seriously injured, and exactly 2,241 civilians were killed in the raids. Nearly 13,000 residences were destroyed, along with 302 factories and 34 churches, halls, and cinemas.

BSA took the biggest hits; the worst came on November 19, 1940, a Wednesday evening, when the four-storey New Building was struck. Employees had been ordered into the lobby and basement to shelter there, but at 9:25 p.m. two bombs from a low-flying German Heinkel found their target. "Suddenly it began to dive and above the scream of the engines could be heard the whistle of bombs. At 9:27 pm, almost simultaneously, there came three blinding flashes, followed by the roar of explosions. The southern end of New Building seemed to rise and shudder and then to disintegrate as the floors and wall of one block collapsed in a mountain of falling machinery, concrete and twisted steel girders."[12]

All told, 53 employees perished, and 89 were injured that evening. One survivor told of a steel girder that fell from the roof, crushing two of his mates; he survived only because the beam that fell nearest him was bent at the tip. Trained volunteer spotters posted to nearby rooftops held their positions all through the raids; some of them were killed too.

BSA produced 126,334 military M20 single-cylinder motorcycles during World War II, making it by far the largest supplier to the British army.[13] The firm began consolidating the industry during the war, too, most importantly by buying Ariel from Sangster in 1943. The transaction did not go off without incident, however, as hundreds of workers at the Ariel factory in Selly Oak went on strike, demanding assurances that they would keep their jobs, though wartime censorship kept news of the job action out of the press at the time.[14] In 1943, BSA also purchased the Sunbeam line from London-based rival Associated Motor Cycles.

Triumph was caught up in the war too. Like the other British motorcycle manufacturers, it sought government contracts for military dispatch machines, yet the city of Coventry and the Triumph main works on Priory Street were hit by German air raids on November 14, 1940. The city's historic cathedral was knocked down from the air on the same night. Hopwood recalled that the least damaged machine tools were moved on carts to an old cement factory in nearby Warwick, while the commercial shop found office space in an abandoned chapel with makeshift corrugated steel walls to seal gaps in the brick and masonry. Machine tools that could be repaired were patched and moved too. For example, a twin-spindle boring machine that had been split in two by the bombing was quickly welded back into shape and was still in use by the company 30 years later — a testament to the ingenuity of the British but also a clear indication why no British motorcycle company could possibly keep up with Japan's leading-edge technology in the 1960s.

The greatest hurdle for the company after the November 14th bombing was in re-creating its engineering drawings and blueprints, many of which were destroyed in the conflagration.

Original drawings were needed to ensure that all measurements and tolerances for future production parts would be constant; otherwise, new production wouldn't be compatible with previously manufactured pieces. Jack Wickes, a talented draftsman at the factory and for many years known as Edward Turner's "pencil" because he drew many of the designs that Turner conceptualized, ran from a cinema when he heard the sirens to rescue many of the original drawings. Other good copies had been maintained by parts suppliers at sites across the country, which helped, but many others had to be redrawn and recalculated by hand.

Government specifications for dispatch bikes called for modest power and utter reliability, the idea being that anybody should be able to operate them, and they must get to where they're going, no excuses. Speed was rarely an issue. Triumph had a weak-performing 350 cc twin in its lineup that even novice military riders could cope with, and to make the bike perform better in the field Turner went on a weight-saving program, consistent with his faith in lithe machines. "I like to keep it slender and light of weight, actually and in appearance as well," Turner once said. "Also I try very hard to keep everything in balance and with symmetry. If I keep them light, I don't have to put too much into the engine to achieve reasonable performance."[15] Turner pared the bike's weight to a remarkable 230 pounds "dry," which was up to 100 pounds less than machines of comparable displacement, but the new frame was not much more robust than that of a bicycle, and a new, tiny, three-speed transmission proved to be fragile. Fifty preproduction samples of the 3TW, as the motorcycle was dubbed, were finally ready for delivery to the war department for testing when the Triumph factory was levelled and all 50 samples were destroyed. The model hadn't been well regarded in house in spite of Turner's public reputation. "Hitler did our War Office a favor," said Bert Hopwood.[16] In the event, Triumph sold other models to the army.

Sangster wanted to rebuild Triumph in Coventry, right where the ruins of the old factory lay, but Turner, then managing director of the firm, strongly objected. The conflict over where to relocate led to Turner's dismissal. "We were in a bad state," Turner recalled.

> We eventually got a few rusty machine tools, rusty from the fire extinguishers, into working order, and a few other companies helped us refurbish them. I had negotiated for a few acres of land outside of Coventry. There was no good rebuilding the factory again because they'd come bomb it again, which they eventually did. [Sangster] was keen on rebuilding on the site because he would get the cost of rebuilding paid by the government because it was destroyed by enemy fire, but I stuck to my guns, and finally when the factory was built he fired me, which he could do because he was the principal shareholder. I didn't like that because I was out of a job.[17]

This was July 1942, yet the friction between Sangster and Turner had been brewing for years, ever since Sangster bought Triumph in 1936. At the time, Turner demanded that if either Ariel or Triumph were sold in the future he would receive royalties on all the patents he had helped to create for either firm. This Sangster would not do.

Turner was not unemployed long, being hired almost immediately at BSA to run its motorcycle division. But he quickly challenged James Leek's authority by demanding control of any patents he might create for *that* firm, which completely soured relations with his new employer. The separation between Turner and Sangster lasted only until August 1943, when Turner was lured back to Triumph with some improvements to his earlier financial package. Still, Sangster would not relinquish the patents. In later years, Turner was to denigrate his long-time boss as "the faceless one who prospered greatly from my brilliance."[18]

The war all but ended in Europe with Adolph Hitler's suicide on April 30, 1945, and in the Pacific with the atomic bombing of Hiroshima and Nagasaki in August. The British nation, if not empire, survived intact, and the British motorcycle industry also proved resilient. Triumph's 500 cc twin, now named the Tiger 100, led the charge in the immediate postwar years. In September 1946, in one of the first important race meets after the war, a Triumph won the Manx Grand Prix (not to be confused with the TT, though usually run on the same course) when Irishman Ernie Lyons rode home on what was essentially a one-off factory special with a stock bottom end mated to an all-alloy cylinder and head borrowed from a generator set the factory had designed for the Royal Air Force. The alloy meant the engine was lighter and could sustain higher operating temperatures. Turner, who was off in America at the time building up his dealer network, initially wasn't pleased with the Grand Prix effort, in spite of Lyons' success, because he hadn't authorized it.

The Manx Grand Prix effort had been the brainchild of number two man Hopwood and especially engineer Freddie Clarke, who was also a seasoned motorcycle racer and knew what would work. The bike had been created even though there wasn't a competition department at Triumph for many years; any specials were built in the repair shop at Meriden, right next to the warranty work. "[Turner] raved at Clarke and was particularly rude to me,"[19] Hopwood wrote, "pointing out that my duties were to 'keep things on an even keel' while he was absent." It was classic Turner — he berated staff for their unauthorized work, then he put the bike into limited production anyway, naming it the Grand Prix in honour of its victory on the island, and continued sales until the stock of alloy generator donor parts ran out.

By decade's end, Turner had further exploited his 500 cc twin creation by introducing a version punched out 30 percent. The new "650" was called the 6T, but that name was short-lived. During a road trip from New Jersey to Daytona Beach to witness the annual 200-Mile Race, he passed by the Thunderbird Motel, which had the mythical bird with spread wings mounted on a flagpole. How exciting, how American, and how marketable, Turner thought. He cabled England immediately and said that's what the new machine would be called — the Thunderbird.

In 1949, as the Thunderbird was about to be introduced at the annual Earls Court motorcycle show in London — always well staged, with large stands, dramatic lighting, and big crowds — Turner reviewed the machine's presentation and decided he didn't like it. "Come on, let's go in the drawing office," he told his publicity director Ivor Davies. There he designed, on the spot, a new, Romanesque stand complete with columns connected at the top by chrome strips and tube lighting, with the Triumph logo at the pinnacle. "He thought it up just like that," said Davies.[20]

Hopwood resigned from Triumph in 1947 — it was almost a divorce from Turner based on irreconcilable differences — and he joined the much smaller Norton as "chief designer." He was ambivalent about the move. Although Norton was a legendary marque and the best of the British road-racing concerns, it was perhaps the most impoverished brand after the war, occupying a row of houses that had been gutted to make a factory on Bracebridge Street in Birmingham. One observer compared the site to a group of tool sheds set in a garden; another called it a "rabbit warren." Inside the close, bleak premises, the bikes were put together by hand on narrow stands, and there was no proper assembly line. Some of the lathes were still driven by leather belts.

Hopwood's primary claim to fame at Bracebridge Street was development of Norton's first modern parallel twin motorcycle, the Dominator. Having worked with both Val Page and Edward Turner, each of whom had built his own parallel twin earlier, Hopwood was, in a sense, a mole. Yet the "Dommi," as it was nicknamed, was at first savaged by Joe Craig, who also served as Norton's engineering director, shortly before its introduction to the trade at the Earls Court motorcycle show in November 1948. Craig, a dour-looking native of Northern Ireland who was nicknamed "the Professor," was a former racer who said the Dominator was "short on performance," and he demanded that deliveries the next spring be delayed until he could get more power from the design himself. Gilbert Smith, the long-time managing director of the firm, intervened in the dispute by taking sides — he fired Hopwood. Yet the machine went into production in 1949 anyway and exactly as Hopwood had designed it, he later claimed. In a pique of anger and injured pride, he also argued that he hadn't been fired but had resigned first.

Hopwood was not long unemployed, and in May 1949 he was appointed "forward product designer" at BSA, a job created especially for him. Hopwood was given a studio of his own with a drawing table and, by request, no telephone — he said he didn't want to be bothered. He was promised complete freedom to create all-new designs. Yet he was quickly promoted again, this time to chief designer, before the summer was out, and he was enlisted to convert BSA's own parallel twin from 500 CC to 650 CC to compete with Turner's Thunderbird.

BSA was an even better place to land than Triumph or Norton. Small Heath had almost become a small town. Armoury Road sported large brick buildings running up and down the street on one side and factory-owned row houses on the other side where many of the workers lived. The main administration building housed an expansive, well-stocked showroom, a dining hall for executives, and all the firm's trophies.

BSA was producing 75,000 motorcycles a year by the early 1950s, making it by far the largest of the British motorcycle manufacturers and helping to justify its advertising tout as "the most popular motorcycle in the world." It was the only motorcycle company in Britain that forged its own crankshafts, and it offered a full range of models. There was the lightweight Bantam two-stroke machine patterned after a German design that BSA had been given as war reparations; it proved to be successful as an entry-level model and with the government post office for telegraph delivery, in which case it was always painted a bright red. A new line of twin-cylinder machines was in play, and the company's premier single-cylinder model, the Gold Star, continued to excel in advanced amateur Clubman road races in England and Sportsman races in North America.

The future of the British motorcycle industry was now set. Both Triumph and BSA were making inroads in the important American market, and Norton was to find its own way in time as well. Sangster, Hopwood, and Turner were seminal names in the British motorcycle industry whose careers stretched from the silver cusp of their initial successes in the 1920s to a very sour ending in the 1970s. That these men worked both for and against each other at different stages of their careers and did or did not like each other should not have mattered, but in England, and in the motorcycle business, personality mattered a lot. For better or for worse, it was the grit, cunning, and talent of these individuals that made the British motorcycle industry what it was. However, the self-reliant nature and even hubris of such men and their cohorts were to prove no match for Japan, Inc., sort of like tribal headmen in Gaul trying to figure out what to make of the Roman Empire.

Chapter Two

Racer's Edge

LONDON AFTER THE WAR seemed more shattered and grey in the newsreels than it was in reality. Often jubilant soldiers were being "demobbed," the lights flared again in the West End theatre district, and the Royal Signals motorcycle display team put on trick riding shows at Olympia, a huge, agricultural-looking hall with a dominating barrel vault roof near the city centre. The featured rider in July 1947 was Geoff Duke, a boyishly handsome man with an oval face, puffy cheeks, and thick, wavy, dark hair. Just two weeks away from being demobilized himself, Duke had learned to ride a motorcycle on a skeletal-looking lightweight Raleigh with a leather belt drive that he had purchased secondhand for 10 shillings during the Great Depression. After rebuilding the stuck engine, then fashioning a makeshift throttle cable for the carburetor out of baling wire, he and two close friends had hours of fun riding the low-powered Raleigh on small-town back roads near their St.

Helens, Lancashire, home. With the onset of war, Duke became a dispatch rider for the British army and learned to slosh through snow and mud and bounce along rutted roads. In time, he was assigned to an army motorcycle Observed Trials team that competed against other posts in difficult, off-road courses where technique, not speed, mattered most.

So it was that Duke appeared with the Royal Signals at the Royal Tournament at Olympia. This was not an Observed Trials meet, more like a circus act, and at such venues Duke would enter at high speed on a high-perfomance, twin-cylinder Triumph motorcycle. With the aid of a ramp, he would jump over several prone soldiers on the ground before landing on his rear tire at the end of the leap. An early Evel Knievel, he had done it many times before. Thousands were in attendance to watch the daredevil antics on this muggy evening in the non-air-conditioned building.

The act had been stuffed into one end of the vast arena on this occasion, however, and Duke knew he'd have to push down on the rear brake upon landing, then slide the rear wheel out to the side, making for a sharp turn and exit. Otherwise, he'd hit a low retaining wall, like in a hockey arena or rodeo, and go tumbling into the stands. Yet a mechanic had fitted showy, extra-long foot pegs on the Triumph the night before, and when it came time to stick the landing and lean the bike over the foot peg dug into the dirt floor, catapulting both Triumph and Duke into the wall. The audience gasped, then laughed and applauded as the chagrined army rider got to his feet, dusted himself off, and righted the machine, all the while trying to wave to the crowd.[1]

Fortunately for the British motorcycle industry, and British road racing in particular, the young rider was unhurt. This was important because it was road racing that restored the industry to its prewar glory in the late 1940s and '50s, and it was home-grown racing heroes such as John Surtees, Mike Hailwood, and especially the good-looking Geoff Duke who restored pride to the average Englishman in a period of declining British world influence and loss of empire. Although he started his competitive career in the rather sedate world of off-road Observed Trials,

Duke was to win six world road-racing championships in all, three on Manx Norton racers.

Motorcycle road racing had its start with the Coupe Internationale, later renamed the Grand Prix of Europe, at Patzau in Austro-Hungary on July 8, 1906, but it is the Isle of Man TT (Tourist Trophy) that can claim to be the oldest continuously run road race in the world. It's an event that still draws tens of thousands of spectators and hundreds of competitors to the tiny island set in the sea between Ireland and Great Britain each June. The TT was inaugurated in 1907 partly in protest of new speed limits on public roads in Great Britain itself. The only rule at the first TT was that everyone went in one direction. If you saw another rider crash, and if you were a gentleman, you might report the incident to a race marshal but were under no obligation to do so. Most years the race has been run on the 37.73-mile "Mountain Course," down narrow country lanes with sharp bends and over cobblestone streets that are as slick as river rocks in the rain. The overall impression is rural, and the skies are often overcast, even foreboding, with cumulus clouds stretching to the horizon. It's a rugged landscape, with little stone cottages in the towns and loose livestock in all the meadows. The race is so dangerous that nearly 200 have been killed in the event.[2]

Many British firms, including Velocette and AJS, did well over the years at the TT, but no marque was more associated with the racing life there than Norton. Norton won the initial TT in 1907 in the twin-cylinder class, leading the company founder, goateed James Norton, to tout his machines as the "fastest" in Britain. When a competitor countered that its machine had in fact been faster on the island, even if it hadn't won, Norton responded with a paid advertisement in the motorcycling press of the day that read, in part, "The fastest machine in the Tourist Trophy was the Norton twin. In spite of misleading statements to the contrary. This is true, a fact and by official figures; we do not perjure ourselves by our statements or advertisements."[3]

The most famous Norton racer was the Manx, named for the firm's successes on the island. For example, Manx Norton riders were victorious in the "Senior" 500 cc class on the island every year from 1947, when the race was reintroduced after a hiatus for World War II, through 1954. Partly what made the Manx Norton work so well after the war, in spite of being a design rooted in the 1920s, was a new, lightweight chassis created by independent frame designer Rex McCandless and his road-racing brother, Cromie — it featured a lightweight but sturdy brazed, double-loop frame and swinging-arm rear suspension controlled by twin shock absorbers that helped to keep the rear wheel on the ground, which is what proper suspension is supposed to do. The frame was designed and raced informally in the McCandlesses' native Northern Ireland during the war, and the brothers tried for several years to interest a major manufacturer in purchasing the manufacturing rights. The opportunity came only in 1949, when Norton managing director Gilbert Smith ordered a test of two machines — both with Manx Norton engines, one mounted in an older "Garden Gate" frame that featured a primitive plunger rear suspension and very limited wheel travel, the other in the McCandless rig. The test was held on parts of the tortuous Isle of Man mountain course called Windy Corner, Keppel Gate, and Kate's Cottage that local police co-operatively shut down for the day. The McCandless-framed machine was decidedly faster. To confirm the result, the new bike was quickly transported to the most wicked race course in Europe, Montlhéry near Paris, where testers wore out two engines, but the McCandless frame never broke. Norton quickly adopted the design, and top Norton rider Harold Daniell labelled it "the Featherbed" because gliding over a racetrack on the machine was like relaxing in a featherbed, he said. The name stuck.

The Manx Norton single-cylinder motor was state of the art when introduced in the 1920s but was old hat by the late 1940s — the Italians were already building four-cylinder racing machines. Expert tuners such as Norton's own Joe Craig and the eccentric Francis Beart (early in his career he abandoned his home in London for a cottage downstream on the Thames so he could work on his designs with solace) kept eking out more power over the years. Beart was a magician who eventually ran his own shop at the historic Brooklands race course, where he would grind cams by hand and then test the machines himself.[4] Later Beart helped to build the Cooper VIIa automobile campaigned successfully by Stirling Moss in 1954 — a Manx motorcycle engine and gearbox sat behind Moss, establishing a chassis design for larger Grand Prix racing cars that was to become the standard within just a few years.

But it was really Leo Kuzmicki, an engineer by training in his native Poland and a volunteer Royal Air Force pilot in England during World War II, who saved the engine. Kuzmicki helped to pioneer the squished cylinder head design (better breathing, better combustion) and later helped to design the engine for the successful 1957 Vanwall Grand Prix car, whose engine closely copied the Manx Norton "double knocker" double overhead cam cylinder head. But in the late 1940s, he was just a chisel-faced ex-fighter pilot with a heavy accent and wiry hair who didn't want to go back to Poland once it fell under communist domination. Kuzmicki worked at the seedy Norton factory on Bracebridge Street in Birmingham as a "sweeper-up."

"When I came in one morning [Kuzmicki] was sweeping the experimental department and we got talking," recalled Norton engineer Charlie Edwards.

> It was soon obvious the man was no ordinary sweeper-up and we were chatting away when Joe Craig came in. He was like a bear with a sore head most mornings and he gave Leo a right dressing-down for standing talking and not getting on with it — and then I got one. But I told Joe that this guy might be able to help, and that he should have a talk with him. Well, it wasn't long before Leo was in the drawing office and in my opinion it was he who vastly improved the 500 and then the 350. He was brilliant on cam profiles, combustion chamber shapes, valve timing, ports — the lot.[5]

The most popular amateur racing machine, or "Clubman" model, came from BSA. Although the company long eschewed official "works" entries in the expensive world of international road-racing and Grand Prix events, its versatile Gold Star model, a 500 cc single cylinder of simple overhead valve design, was to make BSA's reputation for many years, both on pavement and in the dirt. The Gold Star started life prior to World War II as the Empire Star, a workingman's bike, the Chevrolet or Volkswagen of the motorized two-wheeled world. The basic design gained notoriety in 1937 after professional racer Wal Handley won a coveted "gold star" riding the machine at the important but poorly paved and bumpy Brooklands racetrack in Surrey. Handley managed to lap the course at an average speed of more than 100 mph, which qualified him for the gold star.

Brooklands was very important. It was the first purpose-built, banked racetrack in the world. Built in 1907 — two years before the Indianapolis Motor Speedway — it was meant to overcome restrictive speed limits on public roads in England at the time, just like racing on the Isle of Man. The 2-and-3/4-mile course was 100 feet wide in sections and had 30-foot-high banking, far ahead of its time and quite unnecessary for top speeds in the early twentieth century. Yet its architecture was quaint — the green-domed clubhouse and paddock were copies of horse-racing tracks of the day, which served as the only models for its architects.

The first major event at Brooklands in 1907 was a 24-hour-record attempt. With no electric or gas lamps to light the track at night, hundreds of lanterns were placed along the course to mark its inner edge, and bright flares illuminated the rim

The 1937 Empire Star's performance was impressive for a production motorcycle of the era, but it was not, in fact, "stock," having had some engine parts secretly modified by the BSA competition department. Nonetheless, Handley achieved the feat even though burdened by an archaic rigid frame, meaning it had no rear suspension at all, and primitive coil spring suspension up front with no hydraulic dampers.[6] The motorcycle press of the day, which was substantial in Britain, lauded the achievement, and BSA introduced an up-rated, strengthened, and lightened version of the bike, which it dubbed the Gold Star, the next year at a popular price. It had all been a stunt, of course, with a hidden agenda. Rival Triumph had just announced Edward Turner's sensational Speed Twin, and BSA wanted to prove that its older single-cylinder design was just as good. BSA was to exploit the ruggedness and versatility of its Gold Star for the next 25 years.

All but local racing events ceased during World War II; the first major race after the conflict was the Manx Grand Prix in September 1946 (in spite of its name, it was not part of the officially sanctioned Grand Prix world championship series and should not be confused with the TT). Although Norton was master of the island, the firm made only a half-hearted attempt at that year's event, entering a couple of racing machines largely built up from a stock of 1939 spares that had been sent to the island before the war, then stored in a warehouse for the duration. Prewar racing star Ken Bills was selected as the lead racer for the team. "I hadn't been on a motorcycle in seven years, weighed over 14 stone (196 pounds) and was by that time a married man with a son," Bills recalled years later. "It seemed a daft idea, but in the end I agreed."[7] Bills did well, winning the Junior 350 cc class. But lashing rain and swirling winds besieged him in the Senior event, which was won by Ernie Lyons on the skunk works Triumph Grand Prix racer that Bert Hopwood and Freddie Clarke had pieced together for the event.

International road racing really picked up in 1949 with the start of the Fédération Internationale de Motocyclisme (FIM) sanctioned Grand Prix world championship series across Europe. The first event in the series was the most storied motorcycle race in the world, the TT. Thousands of fans ferried across the Irish Sea in the days preceding the June races to drink and party but mostly to watch daredevil riders in a gruelling, even irrational, road course that, on average, kills two riders each meet. The jack hammer bleat of big engines bellowing through megaphone exhausts or open pipes and the burnt bean smell of castor-based motor oil wafting through the salt air breeze were tonics to the visitors to the isle. Riders were heart-pounding witnesses to their own destiny, young men who would try to cheat death on their way to a write-up in the weekly motorcycle press and a chance to stuff their pockets with a few hundred quid if they could actually win the thing.

Predictably, a Norton won the Senior TT that year, and a Velocette won the Junior TT. Amateur riders competed in the Clubman events held as part of the same celebration of speed. Here, too, Norton shone with rising star Duke winning the amateur 500 cc event (even though he was a works rider for the company's off-road Observed Trials team, he got away with arguing he was an amateur road racer).

Duke had begun competing in Observed Trials events on weekends. Trials were slow-speed, off-road events where technique mattered most. Observers (essentially judges) would stand alongside different sections of the hand-marked courses and watch to see if riders put their feet down at any point in order to keep balance — they lost points if they did so. But if they "cleaned" all sections, they lost no points in the event. Duke came to national attention when he did well in the Scott Trial in Yorkshire that year, a historic event that originally tested motorcycles from the old Scott factory against all comers.

Duke described how he studied the Isle of Man course before his first race there. Riding one of his off-road bikes, complete with block pattern tire treads, he traversed the course over and over in practice. "In attempting to learn the circuit, I decided to go over it in three sections — from the grandstand to Kirkmichael, Kirkmichael to Ramsey, and from there back to the start," he wrote. "Allowing myself two days for each section, I set on my scrambles machine and stopped at every significant bend to study the general surroundings, walking back and forth along an imaginary racing line. When a mealtime came due or as darkness fell, I would complete the lap and then continue from the same place at the next session. Endeavouring to remember every bend from the start line to the finish, by the end of that first week I knew in my mind exactly where I was on the course at any given time."[8]

The stage was set for Norton's pre-eminence in the next several years even though ex-Lancaster Bomber pilot Les Graham won the 500 cc series championship in the inaugural 1949 season on the so-called AJS "Porcupine," a 500 cc double overhead cam twin with cylinders inclined forward 45 degrees for better cooling. The blade-like finning for the air-cooled motor looked to some like porcupine needles, hence the nickname.

The unified Grand Prix series was the beginning of the continental circus, as the circuit came to be known in the 1950s. Works riders, as the officially sponsored factory team riders were called, received free transportation to events and a place to stay, plus they usually had day jobs during the week at their respective factories, where their main duties would be to prepare their own bikes. Duke earned a guaranteed 700 pounds sterling in 1949 when he joined the Norton Observed Trials team, then 1,500 pounds as a full-fledged member of the road-racing team in 1950. But dozens of privateers would travel from race venue to race venue, often sharing food, transportation, and even hotel rooms. Start money was as little as 25 pounds sterling for these riders and rarely more than double that. It was hardly enough to pay for petrol to travel from one venue to another on the continent.

The industry overall was cheap. Duke once complained that even as a works rider for Norton prior to 1953 his factory would not reimburse him for a repair to his personal Ford van that he used to transport race machines in the British Isles. When he protested to Managing Director Gilbert Smith, arguing that he only ever charged the company for petrol, the company finally relented and agreed to pay the repair bill. The sum in question? Twenty-four pounds.

Another time, after the 1951 Swiss Grand Prix, both the AJS and the Norton race teams hitched a ride to the Isle of Man aboard a DC-3 Dakota cargo plane in what was also a cost-cutting exercise. The plane took off from a grass strip near Berne in heavy fog, and the motorcycles were lashed sideways inside the plane, while the riders and team managers sat on bench seats along the inside of the fuselage. Duke said the plane was overweight, and the pilot ordered fuel to be off-loaded so it could take off. "The pilot got into a Jeep and drove along the so-called runway and came back and said that will be all right," Duke recalled. "He had the airplane backed up at one end of the runway; then he really gunned it, and he cleared the fence at the other end of the runway by literally three or four feet."

The racing was always tough going and dangerous. Les Graham was killed at the notorious Bray Hill site in the Senior TT on the Isle of Man in 1953; by then he had abandoned British machinery in favour of Italy's more advanced MV Augusta four-cylinder racer. The Italian motorcycles were much more powerful than the British bikes of the era, but their handling remained suspect for years, in part because it was hard to put their power on the ground. Race marshals came to fetch Graham's wife from the grandstand as the race continued without interruption; only a pall of smoke rose from the crash site where the bike had caught fire.

"A seemingly innocuous downhill in the numerous photographs taken there during TT week, Bray Hill is actually steep enough to make a decent intermediate ski hill," wrote one keen observer years later. "And it's preceded by more than a mile of tire-flattening straightaway. Which means top-of-the-line racers . . . are approaching 175 mph before plunging down its steep 400 yards. Only to be faced with the right-hand kink at its very bottom where bikes' underparts gouge out part of the tarmac as they bottom out, all the while leaned over."[9]

Rhodesian Ray Amm was killed at Imola in Italy in 1955. Amm had moved to England in 1951 with a brace of home-tuned Manx Nortons and a van often driven by his wife, Jill, so he could compete in the continental circus. He was so good he was promoted by Norton in 1953 to replace Geoff Duke, who had moved by then to Gilera, another Italian marque, as many top British riders had begun to do. Amm moved to MV Augusta himself in 1955; competing in his first event for the factory, a 350 cc race at Imola, he was killed when he ran off the road and crashed on a tight, rain-slick turn, losing his helmet and hitting an iron fencepost with his head.

Scottish-born Robert Montgomery McIntyre, a former shipyard worker and national racing hero, was badly injured at Oulton Park in Cheshire during a race in 1962. He struck a tree off the course after failing to make a turn and died several days later.

Duke took his share of tumbles too. At the Dutch Grand Prix in 1950, a tire popped, and he came off the bike. "The rear wheel locked, the bike went out of control and literally stood up on its front wheel," he recalled. "Fortunately, I was thrown on the grass verge on the left side of the road, but the bike went end over end down the road and was a total write-off."

Harold Daniell, Artie Bell, Reg Armstrong, Ken Kavanagh, and Ray Amm were all Grand Prix winners for Norton in the postwar years, but Duke was the golden boy, the one who would be voted Sportsman of the Year in a national poll in 1951 ahead of the best football players of the era and elevated to the Order of the British Empire while still in his twenties. From 1950, when he personally introduced a tight-fitting, one-piece leather racing suit to a somewhat scandalized racing world at the annual TT, until he abandoned the Norton factory after the 1952 season over its failure to introduce a long-promised four-cylinder racing machine of its own, he won three world championships (two Juniors and one Senior). He won three more Seniors for Gilera, which did have a four-cylinder racer, in the mid-1950s. Gilera also paid him more than five times what his annual salary had been at Norton to switch, then sweetened the pot every year thereafter, including once giving him a Lancia sports sedan as a reward for winning the world title for the company.

"Norton was a small firm," Duke said. "They only employed 100 or so people and produced about 200 bikes a week — and the market was beginning to collapse as small, cheap cars became available. They needed sponsorship — but in those days there were no big commercial backers as there are today, and by the end of 1952 Gilbert Smith had obviously decided to knock the [four-cylinder] project on the head."

It was a love/hate relationship between Duke and Smith. Both men had modest backgrounds — Duke was the son of a baker and had wanted to race for Norton since he was a teenager, and Smith was an upwardly mobile working-class youth who had joined the firm as an office boy in 1916. Smith was considered a hard-drinking businessman accustomed to getting his own way and was made a director of the company at age 26, even though he had never been a keen motorcycle rider. He became managing director in 1945.

The relationship ended badly between Norton and Duke when, according to Duke, a factory representative visited him at home in late 1952 and asked if he'd scotch rumours that he was contemplating a move to Gilera. For his part, Duke demanded to know when the long-promised "four" would materialize. "I told him I'm only interested in racing where there's a future, not a past," said Duke. "He just stormed off."

Nevertheless, it was the Norton years that mattered most to history — Duke was the last British rider to win a Grand Prix road-racing world championship series on a British motorcycle.

The failure of Norton to actually build a four-cylinder racer, which might in time have become the basis for a road-going sport bike, was emblematic of the looming problems inside the British motorcycle industry. International racing was always expensive, and it was cheaper to keep tuning an older model than develop a truly competitive machine for the future. Yet Norton had partnered with BRM (British Racing Motors, but always known by its acronym), the noted race car engine designer, to build a water-cooled, four-cylinder motor for its Grand Prix team in the early 1950s. Joe Craig was assigned to co-ordinate the project with BRM, but the latter firm never developed more than a prototype 125 cc single-cylinder "slave unit" that would test piston design and combustion chamber performance but not much else. Leo Kuzmicki was eventually brought onboard to help with the design, but it was too late — Norton killed the project in 1952, just as Geoff Duke complained, pleading poverty. One inherent flaw? Duke said that the four-cylinder mock-up didn't even have engine mounts for fitting into a motor-cycle frame.

The much larger BSA factory also failed to deliver on a promised full-bore racer, the experimental 250 cc MC1, a machine variously credited to Bert Hopwood or his long-time engineering assistant Doug Hele. The MC1, first fully operational in 1953, had sensational specifications for its day — double overhead cams and a radial four-valve cylinder head developing 33 horsepower at 10,000 rpm, with a single cylinder inclined far forward for better cooling and lower centre of gravity. The frame and suspension also had unique features, including a kind of reversed front suspension unit that lowered the bike — considered a plus at the time — and an early version of a "monoshock" rear spring unit that today is the industry standard. Yet the machine was never raced. Although Geoff Duke, who tested the machine, and Doug Hele said the expensive project was cancelled only after Hopwood refused to guarantee its success in a confrontation with his directors (an implicit criticism of his leadership), the rascally Roland Pike tells a different story. A well-known private tuner and frame designer, Pike was hired by BSA in 1951 or 1952 after the company either fired Jack Amott, the MC1's first developmental engineer, or he resigned. (A developmental engineer takes someone else's design and tries to make it better but is not the creator of the design.) According to Pike, BSA wanted to race the machine but lost confidence in Amott when he said the MC1 couldn't run reliably at 10,000 rpm, in part because of lubrication problems in the valve train. Although Pike lived in Canterbury, southeast of London, at the time of his hiring, BSA boarded him in one of the workingman's flats it owned in Small Heath and loaned him a new Touring Gold Star that he'd ride home on weekends to be with his family. Yet Pike, too, said the MC1 couldn't withstand the rigours of international racing and blamed the lubrication problems as well, which he attributed to the engine's horizontal tilt. Pike also discovered that the motor literally pulled the transmission forward in the frame, which in turn caused the transmission to pull the rear drive chain forward, causing it to break.

Yet the machine worked, after a fashion. During an unofficial test on a windy, damp day in December 1954 with wet leaves still sticking to the blacktop at Oulton Park, Duke successfully rode the machine to within two seconds of the course record for "250s." Even though he was a works Gilera rider now, he had an arrangement whereby he was allowed to enter classes where the Italian company did not compete, such as the 250 cc class. Duke entered the bike for the Isle of Man the following spring but never got to race it there.

Why? Pike says he (not Hopwood) was brought into BSA chief James Leek's office and asked to defend the project in front of several managers. "I was . . . asked if I thought it could win in the Isle of Man and I told them I doubted if you could even finish in the Isle of Man."[10] The managers cut off all funding for the MC1, believing that losing was worse than not competing at all. A surviving prototype is on display at the Sammy Miller Museum in England.

Norton's efforts in North America were impressive after the war. Triumph and BSA were already building their dealer networks there, but Norton was distributed by a division of Indian Motorcycles, based in Springfield, Massachusetts, which was teetering on the verge of bankruptcy. Government policy required that the cash-strapped country export most of its domestic car and motorcycle production, and a new purchase tax made new motorcycles off limits to many potential customers at home in any case, so North America was where the growth would be. Norton did have a 500 cc twin in production by 1949 — this was the Hopwood-designed Dominator — but it was considered portly and underperforming, both in house and by the motorcycling press, just as Joe Craig had claimed. The company really had only one card to play — a limited production, catalogue model Manx Norton racer it sold to privateers that could be run at Daytona. A victory there would at least build brand awareness.

For years the American motorcycle market was an island unto itself, dominated by long, heavy machines from a host of manufacturers not only from Milwaukee-based Harley-Davidson and Indian but also from companies with names such as Ace, Cleveland, Pope, Flying Merkel, Henderson, and others. British brands were as rare as single-malt Scotch whisky. The first — and for many years only — importer of British bikes was New York City–based Reggie Pink, a former hill-climb and endurance racer who informally brought in bikes and resold them to a few loyalists willing to endure long waits and poor parts and service backup.[11] By the post–World War II era, only two American manufacturers of any note remained, Harley and Indian, both of which continued to specialize in v-twin models in those long and heavy frames. Harleys looked a bit lighter on the fly because they typically had less sheet metal, whereas Indian was known for its flowing, fully valanced fenders, elongated teardrop gas tank with Indian head logo, and often a characteristic red paint job. The two companies traded victories for many years at Daytona and were the brands Norton would have to beat. The English really weren't too worried.

Racing on the beach at Daytona dated to 1903 when automobile manufacturers Ransom E. Olds and Alexander Winston held what amounted to a drag race between their respective brands outside the Ormond Hotel. Later various "land speed records" were attempted on the beach, and they were always well covered in the national media, which treated motorcycling more as a daredevil activity than a true sport. The first Daytona 200-mile motorcycle race took place in 1937 on a 3.2-mile course that ran north on the beach for about half the distance, then almost immediately south on a two-lane blacktop that ran parallel to it. In 1948, the course was expanded to 4.1 miles, also run on the beach, and in 1961 the event moved to the more civilized Daytona International Speedway.

The first race had few if any spectators and only a handful of competitors. By the early 1950s, the event drew nearly 200 professional and amateur racers and about 15,000 diehard racing fans who stood on the crests of sandy berms right along the course to watch the action. Today up to half a million visitors come to "Bike Week" each March for the race and related events.

It was the 4.1-mile course that most became a legend. At an average winning speed of about 85 mph in the late 1940s, it took around two and a half hours to complete the race — if you didn't get cashiered first. Grit and sand could be sucked into the carburetors, and mist from the sea fogged everyone's goggles, forcing riders to constantly let go of their left handlebar grips to wipe their lenses clean with a dry cloth or chamois each carried. Slide-outs and crashes were common.

Norton's first postwar foray into Daytona took place in 1948, when the company sent independent London tuner Steve Lancefield to Florida to prepare two bikes supplied by its small

Canadian distributor. Because Daytona officially was a production bike race, the American Motorcyclist Association (AMA), which sanctioned the event, required that all entries have kick-starters. But true "pukka" Grand Prix racers like the Manx had no kick-starters. In most European races, riders stood alongside their machines, then push-started them once the flag dropped. Norton got around the problem by swapping out the transmissions for ones from its International model, the street-touring version of the same bike.

More problematic was the rule on engine compression. The AMA mandated a weak 7.5 compression ratio, contrary to what one would expect in racing where the higher the compression ratio the bigger the bang, just like in popping a tightly bound paper bag filled with air. Manx Nortons ran a high-compression cylinder head. What was behind the weak compression ratio rule? Harley-Davidson and Indian campaigned old-fashioned side-valve engines at the race, whose inherent flaw was that they were designed for lower compression ratios; in other words, the rules were weighted toward the domestic brands. They were also allowed to enter 45 cubic inch motors, which were 50 percent greater in capacity than the 500 cc (30.5 cubic inch) overhead valve imports. This was done in the interest of "parity" because everyone knew side-valve motors produced less horsepower than an overhead valve model of the same displacement. Yet the side-valvers were no slouches. A contemporary description of the Harleys said they steered well, had good brakes, and pulled hard to a very respectable 7,400 rpm.

Norton failed to score a victory that year, but Lancefield returned to England with information he passed on to super-tuner Francis Beart for the following year's race. One lesson learned: Norton had used special light alloy wheels in the 1948 race, but they trapped sand in the crevices, leading to serious balance problems at higher speeds.[12]

No mistakes were made in the next four "Daytonas," however — Norton won each annual race from 1949 through 1952, three times with young Ohio native Dick Klamfoth at the front. Riding on the sand was tough, said Klamfoth. "It would be soft and loose and powdery after the water leached out of it."

Start time on the beach course was always when the tide was fully in; the tide would recede as the race proceeded. Smart riders rode along the edge of the water because the sand was harder — and faster — there, but the risks were obvious. Wind was the worst environmental hazard. The wind would bring in a biting ocean mist and turn the beach into a wavy and rutted surface, more like a motocross course, which made steering difficult. Still, they'd do the ton — exceed 100 mph — right on the sand.

"With 100 bikes on the course, the traffic was pretty thick, and I just wanted to stay out of trouble," Klamfoth said of the 1949 race. "The Harleys and Indians had more brute horsepower and would pull past me on the soft sand on the beach side. But the Norton had a lot more top speed back down the paved highway side, and I'd really fly past people."[13]

The restrictive AMA rules caught up with Norton in 1953, however, when the firm's newer, higher-revving, short-stroke Manx engine was banned outright because it had not been "homologated," or built in sufficient quantities to constitute a production model. Klamfoth's victory in 1952 was to be Norton's last ever at the venue.

Daytona also attracted BSA's interest, even though the firm, as usual, publicly eschewed any interest in professional road-racing events. Glens Fall, New York, native Tommy McDermott, then 17, had ridden a private Gold Star to sixth place at Daytona in 1949, just as Americans were waking up to the brand. The performance so attracted BSA's attention that the company quickly wangled a student visa for the young man and gave him an apprenticeship at the factory in Birmingham that summer. He stayed at the same boarding house on Charles Road in Birmingham as Geoff Duke, and his tutor was top British trials and scrambles rider Bill Nicholson — the two would tool about in Nicholson's cramped 1934 MG motor car with their bikes in tow. McDermott did well in many off-road events, winning one, but his best achievement was a second-place finish to Nicholson in the Cotswold Scramble, a prestigious event at the time.

"You did it all yourself in those days," McDermott recalled.

"You bought or borrowed the bike, bought your own leathers and were your own mechanic. I still remember buying my own leather jacket in 1947 — it cost $28.50. A helmet was not yet required for motocross, and when you did wear one it was made of cardboard and glue. You wore steel-plated shoes; we made ours out of a car bumper and strapped them onto our 'high cuts.'"[14]

In 1952, Daytona attracted 36 privateers on BSA iron, all Gold Stars, and the factory sent several high-ranking representatives, including competition shop manager Bert Perrigo and Hopwood to observe. The factory clearly was contemplating its options for the future. Yet none of the Gold Stars finished the race, according to one eyewitness. "Every machine broke down," wrote Hopwood, "and to my horror I saw gearboxes broken so completely that the 'innards' were exposed. Not a single engine was free from serious valve and rocker gear trouble."[15]

British bikes overall were considered reliable back in England, if somewhat maintenance intensive. Owners might be expected to fettle the carburetors from time to time or decarbonize the combustion chambers every winter. BSA quality was increasingly in question, though, which troubled Hopwood. If the firm were to succeed in the export market in America, the quality of its bikes would have to be improved. They rode the bikes harder and over longer distances in America, and owners were less patient with repairs, especially when all parts were measured in seemingly oddball British standard sizing, even though in inches, and required differently sized Whitworth spanners. The truth about the 1952 visit, Hopwood later admitted, was that the factory had sent him and Perrigo to America to meet with dealers firsthand over growing complaints about quality and reliability.

With Norton effectively shut out and Indian in bankruptcy, the Daytona 200 presented an opportunity for BSA to reassert itself in spite of the 1952 disaster. BSA dispatched Roland Pike to observe the 1953 Daytona and take notes with a view toward entering the following year's event in earnest. Pike had made his first trip to America the year before to run a series of service clinics for BSA dealers at East Coast headquarters in Nutley, New Jersey, but had been detained by Customs in New York City for several hours upon arrival as officials screened a 16 mm film he had brought with him to see if it contained pornography. (The film was of Geoff Duke on his Norton at the 1950 TT.) For the 1953 Daytona race, Pike again headed to Nutley first, then drove down to Florida in a large van loaded with spare parts and even complete engines. Predictably, people along the way loved his accent, and he marvelled at a waitress in South Carolina who dusted off a teapot to make him a proper "cuppa." He was less happy in Florida, however, where the BSA race team was based in a Hudson automobile dealer's service department rented out for the occasion. Worse, his room was in a motel two miles from the beach itself, which he complained about, and when he was late for a meeting one morning because he couldn't get a taxi in time he was severely chewed out by BSA importer Alfred Rich Child.

Pike believed in the single-cylinder Gold Star, but Hopwood much preferred the newer, higher-revving Star Twin, which he had helped to develop after coming over from Norton in 1949. Pike fretted over the Twin's narrow power band and fragile motor. To convince his boss to take a balanced approach to the race, Pike arranged a side-by-side comparison of singles and twins at the MIRA racetrack — a test Twin hit a top speed of 116 mph, while the Gold Star topped out at 114 mph. Hopwood argued this was definitive proof in his favour — after all, 2 mph mattered in a 200-mile race — but Pike argued that the singles, with their superior low-end torque, would in fact be quicker in the sand and coming out of the turns than the twins.

Pike breathed on both BSA engine designs back in England, but it was BSA ace tuner Cyril Halliburn and a small crew that went to Florida in 1954 with eight specially prepared machines, four Gold Stars and four Star Twins, a compromise worked out with Hopwood. Pike did not make the trip himself that year because he was banned from the race by Child, who was furious that Pike had gone over his head and complained about his humiliating treatment in 1953 directly to BSA chief James Leek, who in turn had rebuked Child.[16]

Still, getting the bikes entered at Daytona was not easy. AMA inspectors recognized the factory-prepared machines for what they were and initially disqualified them, recanting only when western states BSA importer Hap Alzina threatened to get an injunction delaying the race until such time as the sanctioning body could actually prove the bikes violated the rules. The race went off on time. Daytona bikes were supposed to be stock — this could be checked by tearing down the motors and looking for part numbers in a factory catalogue to see if they matched parts used in the race machines. Yet Pike had outwitted the rules committee by tricks such as using shorter connecting rods from other BSA machines — they had part numbers — then machining the flywheels that spun on the crankshafts to make sure they would clear the piston skirts that now rode on short connecting rods.

Among the riders recruited to race the machines was McDermott, the likable young American who had done his apprenticeship in England in 1949. It had been a symbiotic relationship all along, as BSA factory engineers had picked his brain about features of American racing the entire time in England, and McDermott later went on to become service department chief for Alf Child in New Jersey.

Another top rider in the 1954 event was veteran Indian racer and West Virginia native Bobby Hill, whom Pike had personally observed at a Jacksonville, Florida, dirt track race during his 1953 visit to Daytona. Pike was later to write of that event, "Came the start of the big race and Bobby Hill stalled his engine. It looked as if the chance for a win by the number one champion was nil, all the competing BSA twins, BSA Gold Stars, Triumphs and Harleys were long gone. However, the referee motioned to Hill's mechanic to give him a push start and away he went. It was a 20-lap race event and unbelievably Hill worked his way up through the field to win. I had never seen anything like it."[17]

Whereas McDermott had been a teen sensation, Hill was a 30-year-old national champion motorcycle rider, albeit checking in at a lithe 130 pounds. In all, BSA hired eight riders for its eight machines, but the word *hired* is a euphemism. Hill said he was not paid any start money; only his meals and motel room were provided by the factory. "And they furnished the bikes," he noted.

"At Daytona to be competitive you needed a gearbox that

was close ratio between third and four gear," said Hill. "You were always bucking a head wind on the beach. If you lost rpm's, then you couldn't win. On the single, they wanted you to turn 6,400 RPM. On the twins, it was in the 7,400 or 7,500 RPM range. That's what a good rider had to know, what was the top RPM you could ride that would keep the motor together."

Hill said riders were not allowed to take practice laps on the course before the race. For one thing, they would cause ruts in the sand, which would often throw riders from their mounts once the real race was run in anger. "The first time you got to run the course was when you ran the race."

Hill rode that one event for BSA in 1954, on the 500 cc Star Twin, and he won it. The purse was $2,500, which he said was good enough to buy a new Lincoln Continental motor car. In fact, BSA swept all five top positions, and four of the top five positions were on the twins.

News of the victory was cabled back to Small Heath in Birmingham. "When the victory was announced over the factory PA system the workers seized the first piece of metal they could lay their hands on and beat upon their benches in loud celebration," wrote former works director Alistair Cave.[18]

Behind the scenes, the British motorcycle industry was more like a television soap opera, or perhaps "Machiavellian plot" is a more apt metaphor. In March 1951, Jack Sangster announced he was selling Triumph to BSA — no rumours, no negotiations, just an announcement of a done deal. Yet Triumph's fate had been sealed with his 1943 sale of Ariel to BSA. At that time, a kind of option was offered to BSA so that it might, in time, buy Triumph as well. Edward Turner was furious when he read of the Triumph sale in the financial press. He had not been consulted on the Ariel sale, nor had he been told of the secret rider. Now he was not consulted when the Triumph deal was consummated. But Sangster didn't have to tell him. He was the majority shareholder and could act unilaterally. Triumph sold for 2.45 million pounds sterling, and Turner did not complain long — he held nearly five percent of the shares in the company, he continued as managing director of Triumph, and in time both he and Sangster were to take over BSA motorcycles anyway.

And even if Sangster continued to control the purse strings, Turner remained field marshal, as it were. The proof of that came early in 1955, when Norton race team manager Joe Craig and his new star pupil, John Surtees, who was an apprentice and later expert mechanic at the legendary Vincent motorcycle factory in Stevenage when he wasn't racing, came to visit Turner in his regal Meriden office. Norton no longer had a serious race program for a competitive soul like Craig or the cunning young Surtees, then just 21. Would Turner, the most important man in motorcycling and head of Triumph, finally support a full-blown Grand Prix effort, including building a four-cylinder bike to compete against the Italians? Craig could probably bring Francis Beart into the project, and Triumph already had the best British tuner in Roland Pike on its side because of its affiliation with BSA. Surtees would be the rider. Even though Surtees still raced Norton singles at the time, the lad was steadily closing the gap with Geoff Duke and his Gilera "four" when they competed head to head, which was often. Bet on the future, man, Craig implored.

"He [Turner] was totally negative," claimed Surtees. "He shrugged the whole project aside saying it was no problem, Triumph could do three or four-cylinder engines, or whatever, but there was no point in going racing, Triumph could sell all the bikes they made, and more."[19]

It really was the end of an era, not the start of one, for British road racing. Craig was to retire from the industry altogether at the end of the year, and Surtees was to go on and win seven Grand Prix motorcycle championships for MV Augusta beginning in 1957. Additionally, he won the Formula One car-racing world championship for Ferrari in 1964, becoming the only man to win world championships on both two and four wheels. Turner had let the chance slip.

Chapter Three

The Continental Circus

IT FELT LIKE A DOG ON A LEAD, like being a well-behaved dog in a dog show. Jeff Smith, just 16, driving a powerful twin-cylinder Norton Dominator motorcycle on the highway leading out of Birmingham, was being well behaved. His dad, James Vincent Smith, an industrial engineer who had perfected a leak-proof jerry can for British use in North Africa during the recent world war, sat straight-backed behind the wheel of his Morris Minor while its tiny, iron block motor strained to hold a steady 50 mph going down the road. Jeff followed dutifully behind, as he had been admonished to do earlier on that grey, indifferent morning for the long journey to the continent. The air was damp and chilly, and Jeff pulled the collar of his new, waxed cotton Barbour jacket tightly around his neck to cut down the draft. On his feet were fireman's boots, and around his face he wore spiffy Mark VIII "Spitfire" goggles. On his head he wore a wool felt motoring cap, one like all the sports car drivers wore, but turned backward.

The silver and black Norton was a beast; it was a freight train with a light load, a specially prepared competition-grade motorcycle ostensibly on loan from a Liverpool dealer but in fact owned by the factory itself. Jeff would ride that machine all the way from Birmingham to Dover, then across France and Switzerland, and finally down into Varese in northern Italy, where he would ride in the prestigious International Six Days Trial (ISDT) motorcycle competition. Jeff, a short, pugnacious Lancashire native who now lived in the industrial West Midlands, would compete against 220 other riders, national champions and privateers like himself, in a test of man and machine over 1,400 kilometres and six days in length. Almost no other riders in the competition did what he was doing — ride a race bike to the race, then race it — and no other was just 16 years old.

Jeff had been loaned the Norton twin because of his performance earlier that season and the previous year on his dad's off-road 500T, also a Norton product but one with a single-cylinder engine as tall as Big Ben and a frame like a bicycle's, only with thicker tubing. It, too, was a man's machine that real men rode, a machine so dear his dad had purchased it before he bought the Morris because he had to have a motorcycle more than his family had to have a car.

The International Six Days Trial was the real deal. An event begun in England in 1913 and held every year internationally afterward except during war years, the course was always rugged, a combination of fire roads and stream crossings and the occasional fast stretch. It was not a speed competition, but riders had to arrive at a number of checkpoints within narrow time parameters. And, unlike more formal Observed Trials events, riders were allowed to touch down their feet in difficult sections without losing points. "You can beat all of those bums," Jeff's mom, Eleanor, told Jeff on the Thursday morning that he and his dad started out. She stood in the front entry to the family home, the inevitable Woodbine cigarette between her lips, as her son and husband disappeared down the lane to start their journey.

Once at the venue (in Varese), the Smiths stayed with other British riders at a hilltop villa that Mussolini was reputed to have once used. Jeff did well, making every checkpoint on time day after day, and Vincent began touting his son. "Do you know about Jeff Smith and the Norton?" Vincent asked the president of the Italian Commission of the FIM sanctioning body, Count Johnny Lorani, near the end of the competition.

"Yes, I know about him," the count answered while curling his hands around a drink in the hotel bar.

"There's something about the lad you don't know," Vincent Smith said slyly. Jeff was only 16; one had to be 17 to hold a proper competition licence for the event.

The Italian drank from his glass again before setting it back on the bar. "Maybe you shouldn't tell me," he replied, and then he lifted the glass again to his lips.

Everybody knew Jeff was underage, but it didn't matter.

Jeff did very well at the ISDT, making every checkpoint on time on all six days on his way to a gold medal in his inaugural appearance. He won no money, but he had the medal, putting him in a league with only a handful of other, mostly professional, riders. The Smiths soon left for home the same way they had come — the Morris Minor in the lead, the Norton in the rear. But when Jeff eased the motorcycle down the ferry's ramp and onto shore once back in Dover, he dropped the gearshift into first, let out the clutch lever smartly, and twisted the throttle grip hard. He did not wait for his father to catch up; he did not obey; he was no longer a dog on a leash. He rode all the way back to Birmingham at his own pace, very prideful and certain of what he had accomplished in Italy, and he met his mother at home.

"Did you beat those bums?" she asked serenely.

Jeff competed in the dirt for Norton throughout the 1952 season and did well but won few events. In the meantime, he continued to work as an apprentice at the giant BSA works in Small Heath, disassembling, cleaning, and sorting old military dispatch motor-cycles four days a week, while studying at a local technical college the other day, plus two evenings. BSA employed 150 apprentices at any one time, almost all of whom could expect to stay at the company all their working lives. Vincent told his son to aim for the engineering and drawing department apprenticeship — Jeff didn't want to spend his life on the shop floor, scrubbing his fingers and knuckles with pumice stone at the end of a shift, did he?

The BSA concern was not a single factory. An early, Victorian-era structure was built in the shape of a block square with a large courtyard in the middle and towers at each corner, a bit like a castle or fortress. Newer brick buildings were used for forging and machining parts and actual assembly. BSA, more so than any other British motorcycle company, made most of its own parts in house. But the term "modern" was relative — the newest building dated from about 1915, and interior lighting in most of the structures was generally poor away from the windows. Workers frequently had no showers or even cloakrooms to change after their shifts. Workers provided their own uniforms and shop aprons. Paint shop employees could always be recognized by black enamel perpetually under their fingernails.[1]

Billy Kettle, who retired as manager of the spring department at BSA, worked 49 years for the company. He began his career as a "bucket boy" in the 1920s. "I used to fetch the water for people to wash their hands and all sorts of things," recalled Kettle. "I was the odd man out. I used to pick up about five shillings a week."

Nonetheless, a job at BSA was coveted. Pay was above average for the West Midlands, and the company even provided an on-site health clinic staffed by a full-time nurse for minor illnesses and injuries. There was a large cricket pitch inside the motorcycle test track too. Management hosted the BSA Sports Day on the second Saturday of July every year for many years; events included a shooting range with BSA brand air rifles, bingo-style number games, and bicycle races on a cindered running track — BSA brand bicycles were always employed, of course, and the company's racing stars were expected to compete alongside the regular boys from the shop floor. Overall, about 7,000 people worked for BSA's motorcycle divisions during the 1950s.[2]

Most apprentices moved from the service department to the

main physical plant in Small Heath or elsewhere after six months, and Jeff expected to follow the same route. Yet he watched silently as the other young men moved on while he was held back, turning spanners on used World War II machines. His superiors never told him why, but in time he came to understand the real reason — he was competing in Observed Trials events on another brand of motorcycles on the weekends. He didn't have access to any of BSA's trade secrets, and the company wanted to make sure it stayed that way. Jeff was stuck on the bottom rung of the apprenticeship program.

While a factory ride from BSA itself might have seemed a better choice in 1952 — after all, this was Jeff's employer — the fact was that BSA already had the best off-road riders in its stable, which it often advertised as "the five Aces in the BSA pack." Just to prove the point, and further improve its grip on that market segment, the company organized one of the most famous stunts in all of British motorcycle history in 1952. Under the watchful eyes of representatives from the independent Auto-Cycle Union, a motorsport sanctioning body, three stock Star Twin motorcycles were pulled at random from the BSA assembly line and then ridden by three seasoned riders across Europe to compete at the ISDT in Bad Aussee, Austria, that year. Afterward, the bikes were ridden all the way to Oslo, Norway, before returning to Birmingham, always under their own power. The three riders — Fred Rist, Norman Vanhouse, and Brian Martin — not only won gold medals, but BSA also won the much-coveted Maudes Trophy for best performance by a factory team.[3] BSA heavily exploited the achievement in its future sales literature. Even the British newsreels of the day showed footage from the trek.

At the end of the 1952 season, Norton announced it was dismantling its Observed Trials team and wouldn't compete in motocross on an official level. Jeff was dispirited, but not his dad, who finally coaxed the BSA management into taking the boy wonder on as a trials rider beginning in 1953. BSA was so moved, in part, because veteran rider Rist had recently announced his resignation, and top rider and chassis designer Bill Nicholson was about to jump to the auto industry with Jaguar in Coventry.

Jeff also entered faster-paced scrambles events (also known as motocross) throughout the Midlands on his private BSA Gold Star and did well; he could compete as an amateur in these events because his contract with BSA only covered trials machines. Nevertheless, management was watching. One afternoon in 1954 competition manager Bert Perrigo called him into the office. "He said we have a distributor in Holland, and he's asked that we have a works rider compete in the Dutch Grand Prix," a motocross event, recalled Jeff. The European marques, especially from Belgium and Sweden, did better in motocross on the continent than BSA, but it was a market that BSA wanted to penetrate. BSA had some European-based riders it could have entered, but Jeff was told the firm wanted a British rider to represent the Birmingham-based company. Jeff didn't need convincing.

A works motocross machine was selected from the "comp shop," and Jeff was sent off on the *Hook of Holland* ferry across the North Sea. He travelled with another factory rider, David Tye, and the bikes were not crated but rolled onto the side of the ferry inside the hold and simply lashed to a rail. The weather was sunny and mild on the way to Holland; it was about a 12-hour trip. A serious student of history, Jeff had taken a book about the Napoleonic Wars with him to while away the time. For all any of the other passengers knew, Jeff could have been just a young adventurer bent on motorcycling across the continent. Of course, that is what he was, but in a different sense.

"We landed quite close to Amsterdam," Jeff recalled. "A truck came and met me. That was the distributor's truck. We took the machine which I brought with me, and Mr. Flinterman, the importer, came and met me personally, and I spent the first night at his home. He was a big man. He was about the same age as my father, in his fifties. I arrived on a Friday night, and we went down on Saturday and practised, and we raced on Sunday. We stayed the Saturday night in a hotel. It was the biggest motocross of the year in Holland. There's only one Grand Prix each year in each country, and it counted toward the European championship."

The heats were staged on sandy tracks, which Jeff excelled at anyway, and he did well in the first heat, finishing second or third, he recalled. Then the skies opened up before the finals. "Being a trials rider, I obviously knew what to do, riding in slop," he said. "I beat the guy who was the European champion and the guy who had been the European champion the year before that."

Jeff had done it. The 1954 Dutch Grand Prix champion was a young apprentice from Birmingham, England. Flinterman took the lad to dinner in a local restaurant that evening; then it was back on the boat on his way back to England on Monday. Perrigo called him into his panelled office on Tuesday. "That was very well done," the older man said in a relaxed voice. "It was a surprise to us."

If road racing had its "continental circus," international motocross was almost a zoo. Ex-motocross world champion Bill Nilsson said he often slept in tents or in the back of his pickup truck, right next to the bikes, spare parts, and cans of oil, when travelling from one race meet to the next in the 1950s. The next meal would often be a stale sandwich at the nearest train station, or he'd eat out of a tin can on the road, just like field rations during war. If you had money, you'd stay in a hotel, but not a fancy one. It would be deemed a good enough hotel if it had a fireplace downstairs and you could pee in a washbasin in your room without having to go down the hall to find a toilet.

Don Rickman, another top rider of the era who, with his brother, Derek, designed and manufactured the popular Metisse off-road chassis, remembers it pretty much the same way. "We'd be riding in Belgium one day and riding in France on the next day, and we had to drive through the night," he recalled. "We would have a cooker and make baked beans on toast, but mostly it was sandwiches. In France, you'd go down the road and buy some bread and cheese."

The life was romantic; the life was hard. "We never had many spare engines or things like that," said Greeves factory rider David Bickers. "On the Greeves, the crankshaft used to twist a bit. If the crank twisted, the points wouldn't open, and it would let you down, and the gearboxes were pretty suspect as well. On a Greeves, you had to land with the right amount of power or you'd break the gearbox."

A circus it was, particularly behind the Iron Curtain, where motocross was popular. Smith recalled trading a quart of Castrol motor oil to a desperate official for a bottle of Russian wine — each side thought he got the better of the deal. Bickers recalled being stuck for two days on a bridge connecting part of East Germany and the Russian zone outside Berlin. "The Russians wouldn't let us in, and we couldn't get back into East Germany because they had already stamped our visas," he recalled.

And then there was the time Bickers was arrested. "I actually got arrested between Czechoslovakia and Russia," he recalled. "We were on a train, and when we got to the border the train line gauge changed, and they stopped on the border, lifted the train up with big jacks, and rolled in Russian gauge wheels. I decided I was going to take a picture of this, and along came the Russians, and they saw me, and I threw the camera up to my mate in the train. They dragged me and [Swedish rider] Rolf Tibblin away and asked us where is the film? They arrested us with guns and all that. They looked serious. But they were doing their job. It was against the law to just take pictures."

Start money was even worse in motocross than in road racing. Promoters of lesser events would often come to watch the best riders at a Grand Prix, then sign them up for their events — if they had done well. This meant that the Grand Prix promoters themselves had little incentive to pay much start money — the racers had to enter their events just to build name recognition.

Teams representing Iron Curtain countries had it worst of all, though. East Germany's Paul Friedrichs, world motocross champion three years running from 1966 to 1968, rode a Czechoslovakian-made cz two-stroke machine. He was a fierce and dangerous competitor — Smith says you never remembered the riders who finished behind you in a race, but you always remembered the ones who finished ahead of you. He remembered Friedrichs well.

"His father-in-law was not only his manager but was the [Communist Party] commissar," said Smith. "He made sure [the riders] didn't have enough money to run away. He collected all their start money and prize money. Sometimes they stayed in hotels, but often they stayed in tents. We'd often see them out by their tents peeling potatoes and carrots and boiling water."

Motocross and scrambles were dangerous. The 1958 world champion, Rene Baeten, was killed during competition at the Stekene circuit in his native Belgium in 1960. Jerry Scott, a young British rider, was killed during a non-Grand Prix event at Boltby in Yorkshire in 1966 — he had fallen after a blind leap on a fast section of the course, and Smith landed hard on him when he took the jump next. Smith suffered a broken toe, wrist, and collarbone.[4] "There were four or five killed during the time I was riding," said Don Rickman. "There's a big lump of metal going at 60 or 70 mph, and if you fall off in front of someone you get hurt. There were freak accidents when someone's brake lever went through someone's head."

Sweden's Bill Nilsson was arguably the world's leading motocross rider during the 1950s. He won the first world championship in 1957 (the series had been dubbed a European championship before then), and he finished first or second in the annual series in each of the following four years. Only a little older than Smith, and compactly built as well, the two men mimicked swaggering World War I air aces who each tried to shoot the other down but otherwise respected each other because they were so much alike.

"Jeff Smith told me that everyone said to him, 'Stay away from Bill Nilsson.' They knew I was a guy you didn't play with. But I was so keen to get to success," Nilsson said from his home in Sweden, where he still managed a "Speedway" racing team for younger riders well into the twenty-first century.[5]

The Swedish farmboy had originally competed on a home-built motorcycle in Speedway himself after World War II, but by 1952 he was spending much of the scrambles season in Great

Britain because that's where the best riders and best tuners lived, he said. At one time or another, he had factory rides with AMC, manufacturer of Matchless motorcycles, and BSA, which he said fired him after it decided only to support British riders.

Motocross was a dirty sport, and Nilsson was the self-described dirtiest rider. While competing in a Grand Prix event run beneath the fortress-like citadel at Namur in the French-speaking southern region of Belgium in the 1950s, he was in the mix with Rene Baeten and Sten Lundin, another world champion, but he just couldn't pass either of them. He decided to take out Baeten on the last lap by elbowing him out of the way. Yet both bikes went down, and angry fans broke onto the track to help Baeten get back on his bike, while others held back Nilsson. Nilsson got into a fistfight with one of those fans; he won the fight but not the race.

British riders, too, didn't always turn the other cheek. Bill Nicholson, the first postwar British scrambles and motocross superstar, once punched out a race marshal at a continental event when his crashed machine was being hauled away — Nicholson felt he should have been allowed to continue racing. He wasn't penalized for initiating the fracas, but he didn't win the race either.

The most famous motocross circuit of the day was Hawkstone Park, about 12 miles northeast of Shrewsbury, near the village of Hodnet. Long for Great Britain at a mile and a half, the starting line at Hawkstone led through tight, dusty lanes shrouded by overhanging trees and fast, grassy lanes and, most notably, a long hill that rose at nearly a 45-degree angle. It was like a roller-coaster ride, in a sense — the big hill was what you saw first when you came off the starting line, and you could only see the top. For all inexperienced riders knew, they'd fall off the Earth once they reached the crest. The hill was so steep, in fact, that many riders would inadvertently lift their front wheels too high in the air on their way up and flip their machines backward. They could get back on their mounts, but it was usually a losing battle — they'd be sliding down backward all the while trying to brace their machines and work the kick-starter. It didn't help that both the ascent and the descent were slightly off-camber; you could slide off and come down the side of the hill like a personal avalanche. The ground would just fall away from you. The rural venue could only be reached by tight little roadways of the era, yet it easily attracted 35,000 spectators who paid about three shillings apiece for the privilege.

Amazingly, the course featured several pedestrian crossings, and fans sat on small outcroppings of rock to see the race or stood behind cheap stick fencing where they could reach out and smack a passing rider if they wanted to. Bill Nilsson recalls his first race at the park, when a spectator reached over the fencing and pushed him, causing him to crash. Nilsson spent a week in the hospital after that mishap. Another rider once lost time when his spark plug wire was pulled out after it caught on an out-of-place bale of straw trackside.

Average speed over the course was about 40 mph, the range being from 65 mph over bumpy straights to no more than 2 or 3 mph on the "technical" off-camber and rock-strewn sections. Overheating of fluid in the hydraulic suspension units of the day was common. "I had suspension go away," Jeff Smith said. "It would get so hot in the dampers that the fluid would turn into gas. You would just fly about. Part of the trick in winning in those days was to understand the machines and what likely will happen to the equipment."

BSA mounted the most serious motocross effort of any British marque and won the European championship in 1955 with John Draper aboard, and even other makes from Belgium and Sweden often used BSA gearboxes and other components. Yet something was happening in the 250 cc class, where lighter, cheaper, two-stroke motorcycles generally competed.

"As engine design and power improved, competition for 250 cc machines — the category in which the two-stroke came into its own — began to gain in popularity. In 1958 the FIM created a European Championship title for the 250 cc class, and upgraded it to a world championship in 1962," wrote motorcycle historian Ed Youngblood.

The brands of choice were the Czechoslovakian CZ, the Swedish Husqvarna and the British Greeves. It was largely through the 250 class that the importance of lightness and agility in motocross became apparent. Designers of racing machines began to adopt the new low-weight, high-strength materials that had been developed during the Second World War, primarily by the aircraft industry. In the meantime, a young engineer in East Germany achieved a technical break-through that advanced the usefulness of two-stroke engines and ultimately revolutionized the world motorcycle indus-try. Walter Kaaden . . . studying harmonics . . . discovered the principle of the expansion chamber (a modified exhaust pipe), which, when properly shaped, instantly increased the power of a two-stroke engine by over 25 percent.[7]

By the late 1950s, those 250 cc racing two-strokes were turn-ing lap times almost as fast as the 500 cc four-strokes. If their manufacturers could learn to make two-strokes of slightly larger capacity that wouldn't overheat, they'd win everything.

Jeff's machine was the Gold Star, of course, with a "reverse cone" megaphone and a small-bore carburetor for better engine control and a torque curve favouring the low and middle ranges of the RPM scale. His bike made between 40 and 45 horsepower, which would be good even by modern standards, though the overall weight was much greater than that of twenty-first-cen-tury machinery.

By 1959, his personal Gold Star weighed in at about 290 pounds; a stock off-road Goldie weighed about 340 pounds then. The diet was courtesy of alloy wheel rims, an aluminum crankcase, and special hubs. Even the standard foot pegs were replaced by hollow tubing. Although BSA made its own front sus-pension units, rapidly improving suspension components from Italy were being fitted to the works Gold Stars by the end of the decade. The factory also modified the racing frame for a time to let the engine sit lower. The belief was that this had to help the ride and stability (think of a floor-mounted punching bag with most of the weight at the bottom — it's almost impossible to knock over). But it was a chimera — the taller bikes were actually better because they allowed for "long travel" suspension, meaning a bike could go faster over rough terrain and land more difficult jumps successfully.

One way to lose weight was in chassis design. Don Rickman and his brother, Derek, not only competed in motocross on the international level as true privateers, but they were also on to something with their lightweight Metisse frame, which they hand-built in a workshop near Southampton, fitting proprietary Triumph twin-cylinder engines at first, then later experimenting with motors from other manufacturers. The thing about the twin down tube, heavily triangulated Metisse, which in its final development always had a shiny nickel-plate finish, was that it was lighter than *any* of the works machines the major companies were building at the time. Privateers were so successful on it that all the major manufacturers stopped selling the brothers engines directly — Metisse customers had to come up with their own engines or be willing to strip a perfectly good machine they bought new off a showroom floor.

"We wanted Triumph engines," said Don Rickman. "That was our preference, but they wouldn't sell us engines. Then we tried AMC and Matchless, and they wouldn't sell us engines. Then BSA wouldn't sell us engines either. What we did in the end was buy BSA in parts and assemble the engines from parts." This tactic, of course, raised costs considerably.

The old-line British manufacturers did not see the upstart Rickmans as representing progress. They were just a threat to the way things had always been done. BSA's own racer and frame designer Nicholson had long complained about this "stick-in-the-mud attitude of the management," as he described it. "As one example of many, I had built my first bronze welded rigid frame in Reynolds 531 tubing for the 1951 trials season," he recalled years later. "It was much lighter than the standard brazed-lug frame. But competition manager Bert Perrigo and chief designer Bert Hopwood told me to destroy it because the works team were supposed to ride only standard — or standard-looking — bikes. They hadn't the courage to back me up."[8]

Yet the Rickman brothers were on to something, all right, namely light weight and improved power-to-weight ratio. Jeff Smith and other riders, if not factory owners, took note.

"In 1959, I won all the big trade-supported motocross events in England, and I also won the British Grand Prix," Smith recalled. "No one else did that before. Mr. Perrigo called me into his office and said, 'You did marvellous, and we are so pleased. What do you think we should do?' I said, 'I think we should change the machine and build something that's lighter.' He said, 'You've got to be crazy. We just won the [British] championship on a Gold Star, and you want to change that?'"

Yes. And as 1959 came and went, Jeff was absolutely prescient in announcing the end of an era for BSA.

Chapter Four

Mods
and Rockers

I{T WAS NO ORDINARY CAR THAT} stole the show at Earls Court in 1951. Made by Daimler in Coventry, with coach work by Hooper of London, the mile-long, swept-back saloon was a favourite of royalty and dictators-for-life abroad, at least until the outbreak of World War II. Daimler was part of the BSA Group, the major West Midlands consortium that made armaments and industrial machine tools and motorcycles. This particular Daimler was built to order for the chairman of the group, Sir Bernard Docker, and his wife, Lady Norah Docker.

The extravagant Dockers were continual grist for celebrity journalism in England in the 1950s. They bought an 860-ton, 212-foot yacht, the *Shemara*, on BSA's dime and sailed everywhere on it. Once, Norah donned a sailor's costume and performed a high-stepping dance onboard for an audience of Yorkshire miners who had been assembled for the show. In time, the Dockers commissioned at least three more purpose-built

Daimlers, all with pet names — Silver Flash, Stardust, and Golden Zebra. The 1951 car was the Gold Car because there was gold plate everywhere chrome would be applied to standard models, plus gold brocade in the upholstery and headliner. "When I first drove it I expected eggs and tomatoes to be thrown at it," admitted Norah, who had also commissioned a matching dress with velveteen material offset by gold stars.[1]

The Dockers had married in 1949; it was Bernard's second marriage and Norah's third, always to well-to-do men. Bernard was 53 at the time; she was 40. Bernard inherited his wealth and status from his father, Dudley, a successful paint factory owner and banker. Norah's origins were much more interesting. She had begun her adult life as a barmaid in her mother's pub in northern England. Later she worked as a dance hostess at the Café de Paris in London. After her marriage to Bernard, she regularly visited women who worked in the BSA shops and often spoke frankly with them about their love lives, or, as once reported, she'd chat up the mechanics during regular visits to the Blackbushe Airport in Hampshire while her husband conducted business inside.[2]

Bernard, too, was a complex man — his brief first marriage in the 1930s was to a West End showgirl, and his nickname was "Bender," which variously means drunkard or homosexual in British slang.

In 1953, Bernard Docker was accused of currency violations and forced to resign from Midland Bank, where he held a directorship. But his real Waterloo came in 1956 when a representative of Prudential Assurance Company, which held about 5 percent of BSA stock, demanded Docker's ouster. The proverbial last straw had been his attempt to appoint Norah's brother-in-law from an earlier marriage to the Daimler board. And it was Jack Sangster, the brains behind the earlier Ariel and Triumph purchases, then the Ariel and Triumph sales to BSA, who engineered the coup.

"The opening shot of the battle was fired by Jack Sangster at a board meeting on 19th January 1956. He said he disagreed with the chairman's speech at the previous Annual General

Meeting, describing it as 'improper and misleading' in view of the losses incurred by the [bicycle] and motor cycle side in the preceding year," wrote historian Barry Ryerson. "The next major clash occurred on May 2, over the proposed appointment of R.E. Smith to the board. Sir Bernard had already installed Smith at Daimler to look after the day-to-day running of the business there, but the row over giving him the directorship was fierce."[3]

The governing BSA Group board — including Sangster and James Leek, managing director of the motorcycle division — voted against the appointment by a 5–4 vote. Yet Docker nullified the decision by voting for the appointment himself, then declaring that it carried by a 5–5 vote.

The five rebels, led by Sangster, would not give up. They wrote a memo to Docker later in the month in which they aired several complaints, including one against "your attempt to get an official of the company to pay an account for a substantial sum for 'ladies clothes and furs,'"[4] an obvious dig at Norah.

But Docker did not go down without a fight. He bought air time on commercial television throughout Great Britain, demanding fair play for himself, and Norah sent glamorous publicity photos of herself to all the board members in an effort to influence their votes, addressing them to "you or your children." Bernard repeatedly claimed that his apparent extravagance was only intended to generate publicity for Daimler. Had he bought anything with his own money, he would not have been able to claim a tax deduction from Inland Revenue, as he could if it were a business expenditure, he argued. "The large sum in excess of 100,000 per annum which Daimler spent on advertising could be a dead loss if one of the distinguished directors of BSA went about in a cheap car," he said.[5]

BSA had early on wanted to produce a motor car of its own, and the firm bought Daimler in 1910, largely because of its engineering patents and licences. During World War II, Daimler built many thousands of four-wheel-drive scout cars for the military as well as nearly 50,000 Bristol aircraft engines. It was a brand that still mattered in England well into the 1950s.

Ultimately, the Sangster-led faction prevailed, winning over one more convert and voting to oust Docker by a vote of 6–3. The vote was upheld in a very public shareholders' meeting in a London hotel on August 1st that attracted more than 1,000 people and much media attention; the ouster has since been cited in business texts as a good example of corporate governance.

Sangster did not take long to consolidate power. He was elected chairman of the BSA Group in Docker's stead, and Edward Turner was made managing director of the "automotive group" within BSA, which included all motorcycle production and Daimler cars. Turner designed nothing for BSA but did good initial work on a small 2.5 litre V-8 car engine with cylinder heads based on his Triumph 650 performance models. Sangster sold the bicycle line to Raleigh, then in 1960 passed the Daimler brand to Jaguar, which wanted Turner's engine for one of its sports cars as well as increased production facilities in Coventry.

BSA's fortunes improved during Sangster's first few years at the helm of the group. Profits rose to 2.1 million pounds in 1957, and a loan of 2.63 million pounds was repaid in the same year.[6] In 1957, motorcycle sales represented 27 percent of BSA Group turnover. By 1960, that figure was 41 percent, though, of course, the pedal bike division was gone by then.[7]

Overall, sales were strong throughout the industry in the United Kingdom during the decade. Motorcycle registrations soared from 643,000 in 1950 to 1,583,000 in 1960, a high-water mark.[8] The numbers included foreign bikes and, more importantly, motor scooters from Italy, however. Peak domestic production (as opposed to peak registrations) was in 1954, when 187,000 British motorcycles were built. Employment industry wide was at a peak in 1954, too, numbering 13,381. Fully one-third of motorcycle production was being exported, though BSA did much better than the industry average, exporting up to 75 percent of its production.[9]

Don Brown, sales manager for Triumph distributor Johnson Motors in Pasadena from 1956 until 1965, regularly visited Sangster and others in the motorcycle industry in England. As chairman of the BSA Group, Sangster was overall head of Triumph motorcycles as well. "Jack Sangster was the number one guy," Brown said. "He pretty much ran things. When I was over there, he would send a car to pick me up and take me to his apartment in London. He would ask me all sorts of questions about what was going on. He would ask you questions, but you couldn't tell what he was thinking. 'What did I think of the line? Were there any problems?' The American market was their number one market."

Yet chinks in the armour were showing. Brian Slark was service manager for Norton for many years and later an employee of the Barber Vintage Motorsports Museum in Birmingham, Alabama. "A lot of machine tools were from the 1920s," he said. "If you had a man working on the same machine tool for 30 years, he knew exactly how much wear there was, and he'd compensate for it. If someone else would work on the machine, there was no way he'd know what to do. It was just worn-out machinery. It's not like today where you just press a button and everything comes out perfect."

Michael Jackson, another long-time industry insider, recalls similar makeshift practices at various British motorcycle factories. "People would use cigarette wrappers which were probably two thou, and they'd jam it in a machine to make it work," he said. "When the tools were sent to another factory, nobody could make them work."

Parts handling was a big problem too. Throughout the industry, when a part was made, it typically went into a bin, which was then manually transported to another workstation. At the main BSA plant, which in fact was one of the most modern in the British industry, including some overhead conveyor systems, partly assembled bikes still had to be rolled into an elevator and taken to another floor or across the street to be completed.

An industrial film that BSA produced circa 1960 called *The Best of Everything* provides a thorough look at BSA manufacturing practices. Axles for one scooter model were forged one by one by an employee who operated a pneumatic press, then stored in a box for shipment to another workstation. There were some moving conveyors, and there was some evidence of timed delivery of parts to various stations, but there were many necessary stoppages in the assembly line process. Engines were built up by hand, including spinning the connecting rods on crankshafts by hand to make sure they were free and clear. Gaps between critical parts were measured by hand-held gauges. Front suspension units were assembled by hand; wheels were attached by hand too. When completed, bikes were rolled into a warehouse and later tested on a short road course. As most bikes were exported, they were partly disassembled by hand and then well packed into wood shipping crates with destinations from South Africa to Los Angeles stencilled on the sides.

But it was the reliance on general purpose machine tools that cannot be overstated. Machine tools make other machines, and the finished product can never be better than the product you start with. It's often been said that Japanese and German manufacturing prospered after World War II because these countries lost the war so badly — their economies had no choice but to invest in the latest equipment and technology. But it's not so simple — a labour-intensive strategy could have been justified in those smashed economies as a quick fix for massive unemployment. The fact is leaders made a conscious choice to modernize. The Japanese in particular gambled on more capital-intensive, special-purpose machinery, and it paid off. Soichiro Honda, founder of Honda Motor Company, argued that, in order to improve the specification of particular components and have what he called "breakthroughs" in design, he must have the best machine tools available. Ironically, these tools often came from the United States and Great Britain, which were eventually to be his direct competitors in the large motorcycle category.

"The story goes that whenever [Soichiro] Honda said he would buy someone's machine tools they were very happy and kept saying, 'Sekihan, sekihan,'" reports an official Honda company history. "He thought that they were referring to sekihan, the mixture of red beans and rice that is eaten on festive occasions, but actually they meant 'shake hands.'"[10]

Yet British marques continued to use mostly general-purpose, labour-intensive equipment, with a mean age of 20 years each. Labour costs to produce a British motorcycle were high not because the workers were so well paid (though they were relatively well paid compared with other industrial workers in England) but because British machines required much more labour input. By the early 1970s, it was 15 motorcycles produced per "man year" for the British compared with between 100 and 200 for the various Japanese manufacturers.[11]

Don Brown says factory managers in Britain talked about the need for investing in new equipment and conveyors, but the rule of thumb was that they had to recoup the cost of expenditure within one year. "My goodness," he said, "the Japanese already were in a two-to-five-year mode for recouping investment." The Japanese often used rotary index machines that could perform several machining steps in succession, almost seamlessly. But the typical British worker had to stop after any one procedure, then either send the part on to another station for further work or assembly or do some manual adjustments to the machine tool himself before continuing to work on the same part or another part that might come his way. Maintaining constant settings and tolerances, especially in the critical engine and transmission assemblies, was nigh impossible. Also, while general-purpose machine tools had a certain versatility, they performed fewer operations per tool per unit of time overall and as such were less cost effective in the long run than more specialized equipment.[12]

Joe Heaton, a University of Birmingham (England) doctoral student, recently developed his own creative analysis to explain the industry's low reinvestment rates. He noted that low depreciation rates for old capital expenditures mandated by antiquated tax and accounting methods in Britain provided a disincentive to industry to invest in new equipment: that is, tax laws rewarded companies for holding on to old capital investments and punished them for making new capital investments, which clearly hurt their competitiveness and productivity in the long run.[13]

A strict separation was maintained between the Triumph and BSA identities — almost no sharing of parts, for example, and completely separate distribution networks in the United States. Turner, though he was now head of the BSA and Ariel brands as well as Triumph, kept his office in Meriden, where only Triumphs were made. It was a nice office, 30 feet by 40 feet, wood panelled, with a separate desk for his secretary. He did not get up to greet visitors, according to one source — they approached him, and he'd rise at the last moment, then extend his hand.[14]

Turner concentrated on developing the Triumph and Daimler brands, yet the BSA Group owned many of its suppliers (Idoson Motor Cylinders, Jessup Steel, and others), while in many ways Triumph was an assembler of parts made by others, honouring contracts and relationships that predated the 1951 sale. Yet this meant that a BSA motorcycle sold was worth more to the group's bottom line than a Triumph motorcycle sold. There's no evidence Turner cared about this or even understood the different costs and rewards involved.

Turner was not well liked outside the boardrooms in England. A long-time Triumph shop worker once complained of his boss's regal airs, describing him as "this little man with his piercing, piggy eyes." The worker recalled a visit Turner made to the shop floor in Meriden, accompanied by his much younger second wife, a former Australian beauty contest winner.

> This particular day we got word that the service repair shop was to receive a visit from the great man, so we were ordered to do a real clean-up job; no stuff (engine parts or whatever) on the floor under your workbench (he was obsessed with that). We all had to clean down our own workbenches and finally, just before his arrival, take off our dirty overalls and slip on some new clean ones. We wondered at what point we should put on our new ones, but we needn't have worried because the chargehand came scooting round the corner into the shop, his arms waving and his eyes rolling, shouting "He's here, he's here."[15]

Brooklands, in Surrey, was the world's first purpose-built motoring race track. It opened in 1907, before the Indianapolis Motor Speedway was built. At a standard 2 and ¾ miles length, it was longer by a quarter-mile, too. With the advent of WW II, racing ceased in 1939 and the track was converted to Royal Air Force uses. This photo dates from 1932.
(Photo courtesy of John Pulford and Brooklands Museum Trust Ltd.)

Wal Handley earned a "gold star" for lapping the famous Brooklands auto and motorcycle race track at more than 100 mph on a supposedly "stock" BSA Empire Star motorcycle. BSA later introduced its most famous model ever, the Gold Star, based on this machine. *(Photo courtesy of Richard Amott.)*

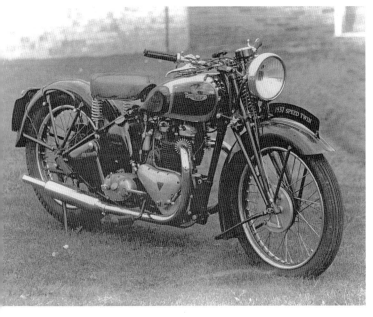

This is the bike that Edward Turner designed — teardrop gas tank, clever paint schemes with chrome accents and good motor architecture. This basic design remained largely unchanged for the next 40 years. *(Photo courtesy of Michael Jackson.)*

The Automobile Association takes delivery of 600 cc side valve BSA models in 1937. Generally speaking, side-valve engines, which operated at lower compression ratios and produced less power, were more reliable than overhead valve models. *(Press photo, courtesy of Michael Jackson.)*

Delivering a consignment of BSA motorcycles in Small Heath, Birmingham, circa 1939. *(Press photo, courtesy of Michael Jackson.)*

Edward Turner (right, dark jacket) and Bill Johnson, early post–WW II. Turner is the man most associated with "designing" Triumph motorcycles. Bill Johnson was the leading American importer for many years.

(Photo courtesy of Clarence Fleming.)

Edward Turner (right, dark suit), Bill Johnson (center, light suit) and unidentified third person, early post–WW II. Turner is the man most associated with "designing" Triumph motorcycles and Johnson was the leading American importer for many years. *(Photo courtesy of Clarence Fleming.)*

Roland Free, a former Indianapolis 500-Mile Race driver, rode this Vincent motorcycle to a world land speed record on the Bonneville (Utah) Salt Flats in 1948. He lay prone on the bike, and stripped down to his shorts, but reached 150 mph. This photo has been widely reproduced. *(Public domain.)*

BSA publicity shot shows American teen sensation Tom McDermott (second from left), BSA team manager Bert Perrigo (sunglasses) and BSA importer Alf "Rich" Child (sweater vest, fedora, far right) at Daytona on the old beach course. BSA's greatest Daytona 200 success came in 1954, however. *(Press photo.)*

Norman Vanhouse was one of three factory riders to ride stock machines all the way from England, across Europe, compete successfully in the 1952 International Six Days Trial in Austria, and ride the machines back to England. The BSA team won the coveted Maudes Trophy for the best factory effort. *(Press photo, courtesy of Michael Jackson.)*

The BSA official scrambles (motocross) team in 1953. They are, from left, John Draper, Jeff Smith, Brian Martin, David Tye, Phil Nex, John Avery and Brian Stonebridge. *(Press photo, courtesy of Michael Jackson.)*

Jeff Smith (partially dressed) during a break in the action at Hawkstone scrambles course, mid-1950s. His father, James Vincent Smith, is on far right, with glasses. *(Photo courtesy of Jeff Smith.)*

Jeff Smith at the 1958 French Grand Prix at Cassel. *(Photo copyright Gordon Francis, used with permission.)*

This is a front view of the BSA factory in Small Heath, Birmingham, circa 1958. Armoury Road is on the left.
(Photo courtesy of Michael Jackson.)

Remnants of BSA factory in this 2007 shot.
(Photo courtesy of Andy Stavely and Birminghamuk.com, Voice of the West Midlands.)

Soichiro Honda, born in 1906, began making piston rings prior to WW II, then organized the Honda Motor Company in 1948. His roots were working class, unlike most industry giants in Japan.
(Photo courtesy of American Honda Motor Co.)

Honda first opened its doors on Pico Boulevard in Los Angeles in 1959. That's a Chevrolet pick-up truck in front.
(Photo courtesy of American Honda Motor Co.)

BSA's Bert Perrigo (center, a former Observed Trials star and race team manager) and Brian Martin (right, a 1952 ISDT star and later a race team manager) with unidentified third person and the iconic BSA Gold Star motorcycle (venue, date not identified). *(Photo courtesy of Michael Jackson.)*

A row of 125 cc BSA Bantam motorbikes as used by post office telegraph delivery boys. Undated photo, but appears to be late 1950s or early 1960s.

(Press photo, courtesy of Michael Jackson.)

Honda won a team trophy in its first year at the Isle of Man in 1959; this image is from 1960 and shows how modest the factory garage was. Persons shown are not identified. A Honda won 4th place in the Lightweight category and 6th place in the Ultra-lightweight category in its second year on the course. *(Copyright Bauer Automotive, used with permission.)*

Racing changed little on the Isle of Man over the decades — they just race right through the small towns. Nearly 200 riders have been killed here since 1907. This image is taken from the Bray Hill section during the 1969 TT. *(Copyright Bauer Automotive, used with permission.)*

Ralph Bryans leading legendary racer Mike Hailwood on their Honda six-cylinder motorcycles at Brands Hatch in the UK in 1965. *(Photo courtesy of Nigel Wynne and Vintagebike.co.uk.)*

Geoff Duke, second from right, in jacket and tie, was the last British citizen to win a road racing world championship on a British machine. He was long retired by the time of this 1978 photo. Mike Hailwood (racing leathers, far right), an equally famous British road racer, won his class on a 900 cc Ducati in that year's races in what was called his "comeback." Also pictured are Reg Armstrong and Jim Redman. *(Copyright Bauer Automotive, used with permission.)*

The BBC broadcast the very popular "Grandstand" series of winter motocross races in the UK in the mid-1960s, and Jeff Smith was the most successful competitor, even after his international career was waning. It's said BSA kept producing motocross machines just because Jeff sold a lot of bikes via the TV broadcasts. *(Press photo, courtesy of Michael Jackson.)*

Motocrosser Jerry Scott died in 1966 when his bike tumbled after a jump and Jeff Smith landed on him with his bike. *(Copyright Gordon Francis, used with permission.)*

Engineer and executive Bert Hopwood (left, business suit) worked for all the important British manufacturers in his long career, including Ariel, Triumph, Norton and BSA. His greatest claims to fame were a Norton overhead valve twin and (with Doug Hele) the Triumph overhead valve triple, but he also had a role in designing some dreadful motor scooters. *(Copyright Bauer Automotive, used with permission.)*

The Ariel 3 was produced by BSA Group and introduced in June 1970, but quickly withdrawn. The idea was that anyone could ride it, whether businessmen or housewives. The rear wheels tilted slightly in turns. *(Press photo, courtesy of Michael Jackson.)*

750 cc Triumph Police Model (twin cylinder) on display at Earls Court annual motorcycle show, London, 1972. *(Press photo, courtesy of Michael Jackson.)*

British media covered the troubles in the British motorcycle industry in 1975, when this picture was taken. Model on display is a 750 cc Triumph Trident, by then made in the old BSA factory in Small Heath, Birmingham, England. *(Photo courtesy of Michael Jackson.)*

Photo was taken in March 1975 at the trade launch of NVT's new models, the 828 cc
Mark III Norton 850 and the 750 cc T160 Triumph Trident. Photo taken at Ragley Hall,
UK. *(Press photo, courtesy of Michael Jackson.)*

The prototype 1,000 cc Triumph
Quadrant hastily constructed by
Doug Hele's development team
in early 1970s. Bike was never
produced. *(Used by permission of
Triumph Motorcycles Ltd., Hinckley, UK.)*

Testing an early Wankel-engine prototype
in a Triumph motorcycle chassis, early
1970s. *(Photo courtesy of Michael Jackson.)*

BSA in Small Heath, Birmingham, was for many years the largest motorcycle manufacturer in Great Britain. This photo, taken circa 1970, does not convey the image of great efficiency, however. *(Photo courtesy of Michael Jackson.)*

Dennis Poore was the "savior of Norton motorcycles" when he bought that firm in the late 1960s, but later was reviled as an "asset stripper" when he took over BSA and Triumph in the 1970s. Photo shot in 1974 at the British Grand Prix at Silverstone. *(Photo courtesy of Michael Jackson.)*

Hugh Palin (right), Managing Director of Norton Villiers Europe Ltd., showing an unidentified person 750 cc motors made in Wolverhampton that were then shipped to the factory in Andover for final assembly, circa 1971.

(Photo courtesy of Michael Jackson.)

Under Dennis Poore and NVT, Norton continued to experiment with a rotary engine to compete with the Japanese. Triumph had initiated the project. Rotary engines have no major reciprocating parts, reducing vibration. About 1,000 were produced, of which about 100 were air-cooled as this sample was.

(Photo courtesy of Michael Jackson.)

High-rise handlebars were known as "ape hangers" in the USA. Rear seat also mimicked an outlaw bike look. Implausible variation of the popular Norton Commando never sold well; some were converted back to regular Commando specification prior to sale. *(Press photo, courtesy of Michael Jackson.)*

"Save petrol, buy a moped," reads the signage on the large display window, but young men really craved the larger motorcycles parked outside. Elite claimed to be "Great Britain's largest showroom," too, according to the signage. Photo taken circa 1975. Pictured here, from left, are Michael Jackson, dealership co-owner Wally Young and dealership sales manager Ron Welling. *(Photo courtesy of Michael Jackson.)*

Can-Am ISDT team photo with Bob Fisher, Ron Matthews, Bill Sharpless and Erik Nielsen, circa 1970s. Team manager and former world motocross champ Jeff Smith, on the bike, helped design the Canadian-built Can-Am motorcycles. *(Press photo, courtesy of Jeff Smith.)*

BSA heavily promoted its great performance in the 1954 Daytona 200 motorcycle race, still run on the beach in those days. *(Poster courtesy of Bobby Hill, who won the race.)*

Generally considered one of the most successful ad campaigns in history. This image was featured on countless billboards and innumerable magazine ads in 1963. The model is the Super Cub, but the bike was generally known as the Honda 50.

(Photo courtesy of American Honda Motor Co.)

Norton Triumph Europe ad, circa 1975. Selling racing heritage in Europe, but it was too late.

(Courtesy Triumph Motorcycles Ltd., Hinckley, UK.)

BSA, Norton and Triumph all resorted to "lifestyle" ads for their motorcycles ads by the late 1960s.

(Used by permission of Triumph Motorcycles Ltd., Hinckley, UK.)

The Triumph name was purchased by real estate developer John Bloor in 1983, after the Meriden co-op went under. He began building new Triumphs in Hinckley in 1991. This undated picture is from the early 2000s.

(Photo used by permission of Triumph Motorcycles Ltd., Hinckley, UK.)

Lambretta was the number 2 Italian scooter company, behind Vespa, in the 1950s and 1960s, but some were made under license in the UK. "Mods" rode scooters; "Rockers" rode larger British motorcycles, some of which were upgraded nicely with performance options, but which often were quite tatty older machines. Lambretta ceased production in 1972.

1927 Scott Flying Squirrel
Engine: 498 cc, parallel twin, water-cooled two-stroke.
Horsepower: 30. Weight: 164 kg.
(Photo credit: John Dean; used by permission of Reynolds-Alberta Museum.)

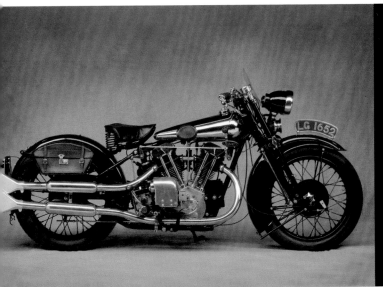

1929 Brough Superior J680 OHV
Engine: 680 cc 50-degree V-twin, overhead valve. Horsepower: not available. Weight: 240 kg. Often touted as "the Rolls Royce of motorcycles." Lawrence of Arabia crashed a similar model and later died.

(Photo credit: John Dean; used by permission of Reynolds-Alberta Museum.)

1940 BSA M20
Engine: 496 cc single-cylinder, side-valve. Horsepower: 13 @ 4800 rpm. Weight: 168 kg. The British motorcycle industry produced more than 400,000 bikes for the war effort between 1939 and 1945. This model, in desert tan, was typical of the breed — slow, but easy to ride and reliable. Mostly used as dispatch and messenger bikes. *(Photo credit: John Dean; used by permission of Reynolds-Alberta Museum.)*

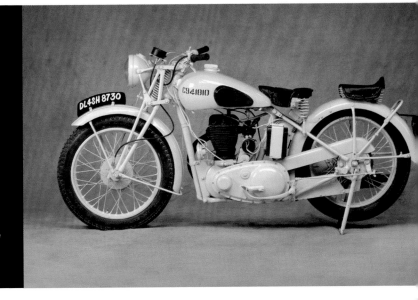

1948 Indian Chief
Engine: 1212 cc (74 cubic inch) V-twin. Horsepower: 40. Weight: 250 kg. The most iconic-looking Indian, made in Springfield, Mass., USA. Note the hand-shift transmission lever and knob to the left of the gas tank and the fully valanced fenders. Too heavy and underpowered, but extremely collectible. *(Photo credit: John Dean; used by permission of Reynolds-Alberta Museum.)*

1949 Vincent HRD Series B Rapide
Engine: 998 cc, 50-degree V-twin, overhead valve. Horsepower: 45 @ 5300 rpm. Weight: 206 kg. Arguably the most collectible post–WW II British motorcycle. Also said to be the bike Harley-Davidson feared most. *(Photo credit: John Dean; used by permission of Reynolds-Alberta Museum.)*

1954 AJS
Engine: 349 cc single cylinder overhead cam. Horsepower: 37 @ 7600 rpm. Weight: 135 kg. Highly successful Grand Prix racer in the Junior (350 cc) class. Light weight and good handling made it work, not advanced engineering. *(Photo credit: John Dean; used by permission of Reynolds-Alberta Museum.)*

1954 Triumph 6T Thunderbird
Engine: 649 cc parallel twin cylinder, overhead valve. Horsepower: 34. Weight: 175 kg. Triumph guru Edward Turner passed by the Thunderbird Motel on a trip to Florida and renamed his popular "twin" after it, or so the story goes. Marlon Brando rode a similar bike in *The Wild One*. *(Photo credit: John Dean; used by permission of Reynolds-Alberta Museum.)*

1957 Ariel Square Four 4G MK2

Engine: 995 cc 4-cylinder overhead valve. Horsepower: 40 @ 5600 rpm. Weight: 193 kg. Basic engine design credited to Edward Turner 30 years earlier. Motor is basically two parallel twin motors geared together to make a "four." In truth, no practical advantage. Rear features primitive, short-lived "plunger" suspension.

(Photo credit: John Dean; used by permission of Reynolds-Alberta Museum.)

1957 Norton 30M Manx

Engine: 499 cc single-cylinder, double overhead cam. Horsepower: 50 @ 7200 rpm. Weight: 142 kg. The most famous Grand Prix racer in the British stable, but the basic design stretched back to the 1920s. Superior handling with the Featherbed frame helped.

(Photo credit: John Dean; used by permission of Reynolds-Alberta Museum.)

1957 Triton Café Racer

This is a made-up custom bike, using a Triumph 649 cc motor and chassis from a Norton twin, complete with Featherbed frame and Roadholder front suspension. Many "ton-up" boys made similar conversions — the Triumph motor and Norton simply were considered the best.

(Photo credit: John Dean; used by permission of Reynolds-Alberta Museum.)

1958 BSA DBD34GS Gold Star
Engine: 499 cc single cylinder, 4-stroke, overhead valve. Horsepower: 38 @ 6500 rpm. Weight: 161 kg. Perhaps the most beloved and collected BSA motorcycle, was popular for years in Clubman racing in the UK and Sportsman racing in the USA. *(Photo credit: John Dean; used by permission of Reynolds-Alberta Museum.)*

1958 Triumph 5T Speed Twin
Engine: 499 cc parallel twin, overhead valve. Horsepower: 27 @ 6300 rpm. Weight: 173 kg. Shows all the classic Edward Turner-designed Triumph touches, including teardrop gas tank, pretty paint scheme and chrome accents without overdoing it. *(Photo credit: John Dean; used by permission of Reynolds-Alberta Museum.)*

1969 Honda CB750 Four
Country of origin: Japan. Engine: 736 cc in-line 4-cylinder, single overhead cam. Horsepower: 67 @ 8000 rpm. Weight: 227 kg. The first modern superbike – better motor, brakes and reliability than the British competition, but not better handling at first. Partial fairing and storage box in back were fairly common aftermarket accessories. *(Photo credit: John Dean; used by permission of Reynolds-Alberta Museum.)*

1969 Harley-Davidson FLH Electra Glide

Country of origin: USA. Engine: 1207 cc (74 cubic inch), 45-degree V-twin, overhead valve. Horsepower: 66 @ 5600 rpm. Weight: 354 kg. The iconic "Big Twin" Harley, fully kitted with lights, windscreen and hard bags. Similar to countless police bikes in the USA. *(Photo credit: John Dean; used by permission of Reynolds-Alberta Museum.)*

1969 BSA A65L Lightning

Engine: 654 cc parallel twin, overhead valve. Power: 52 @ 7000 rpm (estimated). Weight: 178 kg. BSA's flagship and the main competitor to the Triumph Bonneville throughout most of the heady 1960s. BSA pushed its performance twins too hard, resulting in poor reliability. Excessive chrome was considered gaudy by some enthusiasts. *(Photo credit: John Dean; used by permission of Reynolds-Alberta Museum.)*

1973 Triumph X75

Hurricane Engine: 740 cc triple, overhead valve. Horsepower: 58 @ 7250 rpm. Weight: 201 kg. Engine is credited to Doug Hele and Bert Hopwood. Styling is by American Craig Vetter. *(Photo credit: John Dean; used by permission of Reynolds-Alberta Museum.)*

1973 Kawasaki Z1 900

Country of origin: Japan. Engine: 903 cc in-line 4-cylinder double overhead cam. Horsepower: 82 @ 8500 rpm. Weight: 230 kg. This was the second of the great Japanese superbikes, after the Honda CB750 — the other shoe dropping, in other words. Even as the British industry reorganized in 1973, it had no chance to compete with this bike. *(Photo credit: John Dean; used by permission of Reynolds-Alberta Museum.)*

1974 Norton Commando 850

Engine: 828 cc, overhead valve. Horsepower: 60 @ 5800 rpm. Weight: 180 kg. The Commando introduced the Isolastic frame that isolated engine vibration from the rider, but the motor itself was really a decades old design. Considered fast and sleek for the day. *(Photo credit: John Dean; used by permission of Reynolds-Alberta Museum.)*

1977 Triumph T140V Bonneville

Engine: 744 cc parallel twin, overhead valve. Horsepower: 50 @ 7000 rpm (estimated). Weight: 188 kg. Made by the Meriden Co-op, the similarity to earlier Triumph twins is clear. Engine has been punched out yet again, and the transmission is now a 5-speed. Also features a disc brake. Poor sales, high price, dead end. *(Photo credit: John Dean; used by permission of Reynolds-Alberta Museum.)*

Often Turner's engineering drawings or specifications for specific parts or subassemblies had to be corrected, yet no one could tell this to him to his face. Once, he designed a high-performance motor for an elevator lift. It would stall every time since such motors really needed to be low-revving, high-torque designs that would pull hard from the very start. Lower-level engineers just corrected his design without telling him. Dennis Hardwicke, at one time head of the development shop, recalled being given drawings for a one-off clutch that were not accurate. When he complained, he was told, "Oh, sorry, you've been given the wrong drawings. Those are E.T.'s own. I will see that you get a set of proper ones."[16]

In truth, the automotive group at BSA wasn't run like a major company. Until Bert Hopwood's arrival in 1949, BSA didn't even have a dedicated development shop. And, when installed in the early 1950s, it could only have been considered primitive. The shop was housed in a former stable with a 30-foot ceiling and was cooled in summer solely by overhead vents. Roland Pike recalled that an employee would have to stand to the side of the dynamometer with a small squirt can of oil to lubricate the primary drive chain during engine testing, while another worker stood guard over a "kill switch" to stop the motor if engineers began to hear things coming apart. Rather than building expensive sheet metal ducts to eliminate exhaust fumes, the company installed six-inch "drawing fans" behind each motor as it was run.

The company resisted progress in other ways too. When engineers wanted to replace a weak crankshaft bearing in the Star Twin motor in the early 1950s, management vetoed the move because of cost considerations. "As the factory did not want to make a change we continued with the short life main bearing," Pike wrote.[17]

BSA motorcycle handling was highly regarded in the trade, however, thanks in part to master tuners such as Roland Pike and frame designers such as Bill Nicholson. Triumph could make no such claim in the 1950s. It was said you didn't ride a Triumph around a bend, you wrestled it in the corners. Some Triumph road bikes of the era were known for flexing under hard riding and dangerous head shaking at high speed. "Handles like a pregnant camel with a hinge in the middle" was just one of sundry ditties told about the frames at the time. Road testing in those days was informal but direct — the factories just gave the bikes to a couple of chaps and told them to ride to London and back and report what they found. At Triumph, test riders were provided with waxed cotton Barbour and Belstaff suits for free (they were under testing from their respective manufacturers), but the riders had to supply their own boots, goggles, and gloves. To prove they had made the run, a North London post office stamped rider cards.[18]

It was because of the firm's (and Turner's) lax attitude toward handling in its production bikes that the so-called Triton emerged — private tuners simply took the lusty, beautifully styled Triumph 650 cc motors and installed them in better-handling Norton Featherbed frames. Only after a competitor in the annual Big Bear Run off-road race in America was killed when his new Triumph double down tube frame fractured just below the steering head did the company take the problem seriously. As news of the tragedy reached Meriden, "[Turner] came down the corridor from his office and into experimental, his face as black as thunder and wanting to know why the frame had fractured," recalled one veteran Triumph employee.[19]

Improvements were made on a trial-by-error basis — two similar frames were taken to a nearby racetrack, modified on the fly, then ridden to the limits by a very brave factory rider. At what speed would it shake? Wobble? Break? In the end, the company decided that the double down tube frame with an added top rail would suffice.

Percy Tait, the lead Triumph test rider and a successful road racer in the 1950s and '60s, described arguing with development engineer Doug Hele about a mid-'60s frame. Hele understood handling and was well liked by staff because he would listen, but he had to be convinced he was wrong. The particular dispute on this day was which steering head angle gave the best handling. "To prove a point, I took Doug to a lane near the factory where there was a super left-hander with bumps," said Tait. "I got him to lie on the verge so he could study what happened as I came through. I rode 'my' frame first and went through just great. Then I tried it on the other one, got a wobble on, and saw Doug doing a handstand into the ditch. He thought I was going to come off and hit him."[20]

There was one thing the British did right in the 1950s, however. They got into the North American market just as American postwar affluence and recreational motorcycle use were emerging. The BSA brand entered the North American market in 1945, working with English ex-patriate Alfred Rich Child. Born in Chichester in 1891, Child had attended Greenwich Naval Academy during World War I but had not joined the navy himself due to poor vision. His father had apprenticed him to a corn broker, which had been unacceptable to Alf. He soon booked passage on a Cunard liner to New York, working as a mess steward to help pay his way. With the outbreak of war in Europe, he joined the U.S. Coast Guard searching ships for embargoed products destined for Germany.

After the war, Child took a job with David Weistrich, an ex-patriate English Jew who owned a wholesale bicycle parts supply business in New York City. When Weistrich fell ill, Child hoped to take over day-to-day management of the firm, but that role fell to Weistrich's brother-in-law, and Child left the company. He soon approached Arthur Davidson about selling for the Harley-Davidson motorcycle company. Child already owned a Harley and knew the brand well. Davidson took him on but only after insisting that Rich prove he wasn't Jewish.[21]

Davidson liked the young man's affability, daring, and good knowledge of motorcycles. "The Motor Company," as Harley-Davidson came to style itself, made Child a sales rep throughout the Deep South in 1920 and in 1922 sent him to Capetown, South Africa, where he began an eight-month epic journey travelling up to Cairo on a Harley v-twin sidecar rig. It was a quest tracking down rumours of dealerships and travelling across dusty savannas with no roads in sight. In Uganda, for example, he employed local tribesmen to make a temporary ferry by spanning logs on their shoulders between two columns of men, then carrying the sidecar rig on the logs.[22]

In 1924, Child was sent to Japan to investigate sales of Harley-Davidson to that still mysterious land. Independent importers had purchased a few dozen examples over the years, but Harley wanted a proper dealer network with full spares support. Child established the Harley-Davidson Sales Company of Japan, garnering a 5 percent commission for himself based on the "landed cost" of all machines, which ultimately made him a reasonably wealthy man. "Early in 1924, with a firm agreement with Harley-Davidson in my briefcase, and with my wife and daughter and a few belongings, I returned to Tokyo and set about the job of planning the sale of 350 Harley-Davidsons and the $20,000 worth of spare parts, which I had left in the hands of Harry Devine, the parts manager, who, with more than twenty years of experience in the demand for individual spares, made a most excellent selection," Child wrote in 1977. "Harry also developed blue prints to construct, in Japan, wooden bins to hold the different sizes of parts, with his expert knowledge of the quantities of each part required for the sizes of each individual bin. Carpentry being one of Japan's specialties at the time, these bins were built in Philippine mahogany in advance of the arrival of the parts from Milwaukee."[23]

The worldwide economic crash of 1929 combined with a major devaluation of the yen made it hard to sell Milwaukee-made bikes in Japan, however, so Child helped local business interests to obtain manufacturing rights to make the heavy side-valve twins in Japan, complete with all necessary engineering drawings and heat-treating secrets. The deal worked well enough until 1936, when the Japanese Harley factory was seized by the investors with government backing. Production continued for many years under the Rikuo name (it meant "King of the Road," the Harley nickname in Japan), and no further royalties were paid to the parent company. Child formed a new trading business to import genuine Harleys from Milwaukee to compete, but a nearly tenfold increase in tariffs in 1937 put him out of business, and he returned to America.[24]

It was full circle for the native Englishman in 1944 when Child sailed to England and met with Edward Turner and Jack

Sangster, seeking Triumph distribution rights in North America. The two moguls demurred, sticking with Bill Johnson instead, but Child returned the next year and met with BSA motorcycle chief James Leek, wangling rights to distribute BSA and Sunbeam motorcycles in North America.

Bert Hopwood, then at Triumph but not unaware of developments in Birmingham, marvelled at Child's unannounced visit to Small Heath before the war had actually ended, and he describes Child as "an American" in his autobiography. Apparently, all those years living in North America and Japan had completely eroded his accent. "With a 5-year agreement in his pocket Alf Child sailed back to the USA from Fowey in Cornwall in a Liberty ship laden with china clay, which sank after colliding with an oil tanker off the US coast," wrote Hopwood. "Fortunately for BSA, Child was hauled from the sea and typical of the man, was, next day, setting up office in New York. He started operating from a small hotel room but he quickly went on to build a huge and efficient dealer structure which, by 1949, was operating smoothly from two distributor centers."[25]

Child sold West Coast distribution rights to Indian Motorcycle distributor L.R. "Hap" Alzina in 1949, who increased the dealer network in California and nearby states from 3 to almost 250 in the next 15 years. Child retained his Nutley, New Jersey, offices for several more years, hiring former boy racer and informal BSA apprentice Tommy McDermott as his service manager on the recommendation of BSA chiefs back in England, and he continued to build up dealers along the East Coast. "If he had a dealer that sold 10 motorcycles a year, he was a hero," recalled McDermott, who in later years opened his own Harley-Davidson dealership in upstate New York.

With rare exceptions, dealerships in America at least until the arrival of Honda in the early 1960s were off in a corner of a hardware store, tire repair shop, or appliance store. Sometimes an eager motorcycle club member would be granted a franchise if he bought a bike for himself and ordered a couple extra plus a spares kit for sale to other club members throughout the coming riding season.

"We had a dealer in the [San Francisco] Bay Area called Pelican Dives," recalled Norton's Brian Slark. "On one side of the store was diving equipment, and the other side was a couple of motorcycles. Yeah — if you could go to a small town and sell the guy three motorcycles and a sign, yeah, you had a dealer."

Edward Turner had done well to link up with Bill Johnson. Johnson Motors, or JoMo as it came to be called, was different, especially when it relocated to a spacious former luxury automobile dealership after the war. The new showroom featured a tall glass façade, polished tile floor, well-stocked parts department arranged like library stacks, and six hydraulic lifts. It was first class in every way and unlike anything the American motorcycle community had seen before.

"Bill Johnson and Edward Turner were big buddies," recalled Don Brown. "When Edward would come to see Johnson Motors, he was really coming to see Bill Johnson. He had one of those big fishtail Cadillacs, and Bill would get one off the lot and drive the two of them around. Sometimes Edward would like to go around and visit dealers. They wouldn't know he was coming. That would scare them half to death."

Yet Turner was beginning to regret the exclusive deal he had made with Johnson prior to the war — the spontaneous, optimistic American just wasn't expanding the dealer network fast enough. Turner arranged to buy back distribution rights for the East Coast and Midwest and base a new company, Triumph Corporation of America, near Baltimore in 1951. English ex-patriate Denis McCormack was chosen to head the company. The operation was so successful, and the threat of increased British penetration of the American motorcycle market so real, that Harley-Davidson petitioned the United States Tariff Commission the following year, accusing the Brits of selling their machines in America at prices lower than in Great Britain itself. This probably was true, though different tax codes and supply-and-demand issues complicated the matter. Representatives from BSA and Triumph, which were run as completely separate companies, argued that Harley had no comparably sized middleweight bikes of its own for sale, so what the British were doing was of no concern to the American company. The tariff commission ruled for the British, and it was not until 1957 that Harley-Davidson introduced its own middleweight bike, the popularly named Sportster.

Don Brown was an important hire for Johnson Motors in 1956. A young army veteran and Triumph Thunderbird enthusiast, Brown hosted a California radio show in the 1950s that covered the local motorcycle scene. Johnson was a guest one evening; he was so impressed with Brown's knowledge and verve that he hired him on the spot. Brown extended JoMo's dealer network from 84 to more than 350 in a 19-state territory between 1956 and 1965, when he moved to BSA's distributor in Nutley.

Johnson and Turner also resorted to stunts to sell motorcycles. Both men gave away motorcycles to actors in America and England in exchange for photo rights (Brown says up-and-coming actor Steve McQueen demanded a free machine in exchange for photo rights, then agreed to a discounted purchase price because he wasn't a big enough star yet). Setting "world records" was another trick. It wasn't much different from boxers and wrestlers of the era who often held multiple world championships. In September 1955, Johnny Allen streaked across the Bonneville Salt Flats in Utah on a fully faired 650 cc Triumph Thunderbird at 193.72 MPH, touted as a new "world land speed record." The international sanctioning body, the FIM, refused to recognize the record because the American sanctioning body that had observed the event, the American Motorcycle Association, wasn't an affiliate. Allen broke his own record the following year, taking the same bullet-shaped Triumph up to 214.72 MPH. Again the FIM refused to recognize the record, but it mattered not to Turner, who ordered the factory to begin sticking labels on its machines featuring a simple drawing of a Thunderbird and proclaiming that Triumph was the world's fastest motorcycle. In 1959, the factory introduced its most popular model ever, the twin-carburetor Bonneville.

Motorcycle land speed records were always effective in garnering publicity in the North American market at relatively little cost, and they fit in well with the daredevil image the industry both loved and hated. Another British manufacturer, Vincent, had set the record at Bonneville in 1948. The Vincent machine, a 1,000 cc overhead valve Black Lightning v-twin said to be the bike Harley-Davidson most feared, was piloted by ex-Indianapolis 500 racer Rollie Free. In claiming the record at 150.313 MPH, Free gave the world one of the most famous motorcycle images ever. Forty-seven at the time, Free wore a bucket-style helmet, tight swim trunks, and beach sandals — and nothing else — as he lay prone over the motorcycle, his abdomen resting directly on the rear fender and his chest right on the gas tank. There was no seat, no streamlining, and no front fender on the bike.

Norton was imported from the mid-1950s to the early '60s by the Indian Trading Company, best described as an offshoot of the Indian motorcycle company in Springfield, Massachusetts, but really under the control of a British concern that also sold Royal Enfield motorcycles in North America. In spite of its legendary racing successes, Norton sold only "four or five machines annually" in America during this period, according to Bert Hopwood, who was back at the helm of Norton in 1956. Even if the extremely low estimate must be considered more of an insult than an accurate tally, it is true that Norton street bikes were rare in the United States at the time. In time, Hopwood came to question why the Bracebridge Street factory in Birmingham bothered with the Manx Norton racer, which sold between 80 and 100 a year worldwide during this period. The bike cost between 400 and 500 pounds at the time and was profitable, yet the purchase price equalled a full year's salary for the average workingman in England. Hopwood wanted to end production of the Manx, and he complained that too many Norton engineers were wasting their time tweaking a dead-end design when they should have been working on new, mass-market models. He got his wish in one regard — Manx Norton production finally ended in 1963.

Sales for Norton improved only in the 1960s when Joe and Mike Berliner, Jewish-American immigrant brothers, took over distribution in the United States. Berliner Motor Corporation simply bought the bikes from the factory and then resold them.

The Berliners assumed all responsibility for distributing and advertising the bikes too. Yet it was an uphill battle bringing the bikes to market — Hopwood recalled with dismay that Joe Berliner was stood up when he came to London to visit the chairman of Associated Motor Cycle Group (AMC), which owned the important Norton, Matchless, and AJS brands at the time, as well as James and Frances-Barnett. "I always wanted to see Plumstead Road, Woolwich [home to AMC]," Berliner told Hopwood. "Now we will recuperate by having lunch at the Ritz."[26]

The Berliners, like Bill Johnson before them, were part businessmen and part showmen. They also imported the Ducati brand and in the early 1960s convinced the Italian factory to build a four-cylinder, 1,260 cc working prototype to compete head-on with the Harley-Davidson Big Twin motorcycles. The Berliners coveted the important police bike market in the United States, which Harley virtually owned. Even though government contracts for motorcycle purchases typically required an open bidding process, requirements often included such pro-Harley specifications as five-inch-wide tires or demanded motors "larger than 1,200 cc," which automatically meant Harley-Davidson. Two working prototypes of the Apollo were built at the brothers' behest though never marketed.[27]

Where the British industry stumbled badly was in response to the Italian scooter craze of the 1950s. Vespa (Italian for wasp) and Lambretta became the stylish choice of young commuters across Europe and were popular in England too. This was the era of the "mods and rockers," and the mods liked scooters, often festooned with extra lights and chrome bits. The mods tended to be more middle-class youth and often dressed in suits, while the rockers had a grittier, working-class reputation and preferred rorty, powerful, full-sized, Made-in-England motorcycles. They wore leather motorcycle jackets straight out of Marlon Brando's *The Wild One* and slicked their hair with pomade just like American "greasers." The rockers were rooted in the so-called "ton-up boys," serious motorcyclists who rode hopped-up

British iron and congregated most famously at the Ace Café, an all-night truck stop on the North Circular Road in London in the late 1950s. Those boys would challenge each other to ride up to and back from a distant signpost, including time to kick-start the bikes from cold, before a 45 RPM record from the café's juke box finished, or a couple of mates would race south to Brighton, about an hour down and another hour back up. The most daring would make the all-night run north to Scotland. British media accounts of the trend, including graphic coverage of high-speed crashes, helped to build the legend.

"We were lunatics, taking lifts here and there, riding at 100 MPH without crash helmets," recalled former Ace customer Jan Turner, who often rode pillion on a boyfriend's bike. "My parents don't know to this day what I was up to. I certainly wouldn't like my daughter to do what I did back then."[28]

Recalled Barry Cheese, an Ace regular from 1957 through 1963 who went by the *nom de guerre* Noddy, "A couple of traffic cops [once] told me to pull over. I said, 'Not today, thanks,' and took off, giving it full-stick up and down the North Circular. But I had to give myself up, otherwise my mate would have got the blame — they'd got the numberplate."[29]

Sidney Furie's *The Leather Boys*, released in 1964 and filmed partly at the Ace Café, aptly portrays the times. It's about two working-class mates who save all their pennies and spend their free time fixing up their motorcycles, and it includes a surprising subplot dealing with one biker's homosexual affection for the other. The lead female role went to Rita Tushingham, who also played Zhivago's daughter in *Dr. Zhivago*. She rode pillion on a BSA 650 in *The Leather Boys*. The 1979 release *Quadrophenia*, co-starring Sting, focuses more on the social contrast between mods and rockers and re-creates a legendary "punch-up" between the two groups at Brighton.

The British manufacturers made all the hardware that both ton-up boys and rockers rode, but they rode secondhand equipment more often than not. The manufacturers really coveted the more well-to-do mod crowd. Velocette introduced the Viceroy in 1960. Unusual in design, it featured a twin-cylinder motor, electric start, and flowing fender lines — all in all, a charmer. But like all Velocette products, it was priced higher than the competition and did not do well. Velocette never recouped its tooling costs for the all-new design.

The Triumph Tigress, also sold as the BSA Sunbeam, came in 175 cc two-stroke and 250 cc twin-cylinder four-stroke versions. The 250 had good suspension for a scooter, but handling was compromised by the inevitable 10-inch wheels required to make it a scooter. Nor were the machines attractive — the sheet metal was very bulbous, much more like a fat person than a svelte model — and build quality overall was suspect.

Even as sales stagnated for the Tigress (it was discontinued in 1965), Triumph launched another scooter, the 100 cc Tina, in 1963. Its claim to fame was an automatic transmission patented by Edward Turner. Just before launch, Turner assembled his senior staff on the lawn in front of the Meriden factory and presented them with machines painted in six differing colours. As the machine was to be targeted to women (many ads for it featured a woman on the seat with the words "It almost drives itself."), one staffer suggested that female employees be invited down to choose colours. "Get some girls," Turner snorted, but when production actually began he stuck to the colours he had initially chosen.[30] Like the Tigress, the Tina also wasn't successful in the marketplace and was soon discontinued.

BSA had actually attempted to enter the scooter market in a timely fashion in 1955 with the prototype 70 cc Dandy two-stroke and the more impressive 198 cc four-stroke, shaft-driven, electric start Beeza that looked a lot like a Lambretta. Both projects were doomed as an alloy cylinder specified in the original design of the Dandy was scrapped in favour of a lower-cost iron cylinder, which led to overheating, while the Beeza suffered from cost and reliability issues. Few samples of the Beeza were produced, and the Dandy was soon withdrawn following very limited sales. Bert Hopwood, as chief designer at BSA during development of the machines, was often blamed for these expensive failures, and he writes very defensively about the project in his autobiography — as usual, everyone but himself made mistakes.

AMC also introduced a scooter, the James, featuring a 250 cc two-stroke motor and small steel wheels. It, too, flopped. They all flopped.

Road racing remained popular in England, and British riders continued to dominate, both on the isles and often in Europe, though not on British machinery by the late 1950s. Geoff Duke won three more world championships after he moved to Gilera in 1953, but he never won the championship again after supporting a riders' strike at the 1955 Dutch Grand Prix.

The Dutch Grand Prix routinely drew 100,000 visitors to the road course in Assen and was a moneymaker for its organizers, the KNMV (the Royal Dutch Motorcyclists Association). It also paid the lowest start money on the Grand Prix circuit — 25 pounds. Privateers had been complaining about the low amount for years, which amounted to barely half of what they received elsewhere. Finally, in 1955, 12 British and Australian riders said they'd start the race but pull out after one lap if they didn't get a meeting with organizers first to discuss the matter. The organizers refused, and the riders indeed pulled out after one lap, returning to the paddock in front of a stunned crowd. Although the motivation was different, the riders anticipated by exactly 50 years the Formula 1 strike at Indianapolis when most drivers pulled out after one lap because of tire safety concerns. The 1955 motorcyclists also threatened to pull out of the premier 500 cc race, run later in the day, if they didn't get their raise. To prevent chaos, Gilera works riders Duke and Reg Armstrong along with MV rider Umberto Masetti approached the organizers and worked out a compromise; the riders would be paid an extra 20 pounds each, and the Senior race went off without a hitch.

That should have ended the matter, but it didn't. On November 24, 1955, something called the International Sporting Committee of the FIM held an extraordinary session in London. It was a trial of sorts, with a panel that included three of the Assen race stewards. They were called not as witnesses but as judges. Duke (nattily dressed as always; he often wore tweedy coats over dark trousers), Armstrong, and two other riders were invited to attend. They were unsuspecting; they thought this was an inquiry into what had happened at the race that summer, but a trial it was. They were given the charges against them only two hours before the start of the meeting. It was all held in private; the press was barred at the door.

The rump court's ruling turned Solomon's logic on its head. The committee's chairman, Emil Vorster, ruled that the privateers couldn't be punished for pulling out of the 350 cc race — after all, they did start the race, and that's all they were being paid for. This led to howls from some observers after the decision was revealed as spectators and competitors alike go to a "race," not to a "start." Yet Duke, Armstrong, and the 12 privateers were suspended for six months each, starting January 1, 1956, for allegedly threatening not to race in the Senior; Masetti received a four-month suspension. Vorster, supported by all but one on the panel, ruled that the alleged threat to disrupt the 500 cc race was the far more serious crime. Duke never acknowledged that he was party to the threat, only that he tried to work out a compromise. The British Auto-Cycle Union immediately protested this ruling to the FIM, the supreme authority on racing, to no avail, and Duke and Armstrong served their sentences on the sidelines, which forced them to miss half the Grand Prix season in 1956. Armstrong retired from racing altogether at the end of the year, and Duke, the most famous motorcycle road racer in British history up to that time, was never to win a world championship again, being effectively eclipsed in time by a new, younger British racing sensation named John Surtees. "Clearly, we were set up as an example to deter any other FIM-licence holders from contemplating similar protest action in the future," Duke said.

Chapter Five

The Last World Champion

WHEN THE NINE SMALL MEN — eight obviously from Asia and one sounding very much like a Yankee — disembarked at London's Gatwick Airport that mild spring morning in May 1959, curious customs agents looked them over from tip to toe, thumbed through their travel documents, and sifted through their luggage. The documents looked OK — they indicated the men were employees of the Okura Trading Company — but the agents were surprised to find an assortment of spark plugs, pistons, and camshafts stuffed between shirts and trousers and underwear in their luggage.

Who are you really? the confused British agents asked. What is this stuff?

Almost no one in England had seen a Japanese motorcycle before, let alone a Japanese motorcycle road racer. Yet that's who these people were — riders Gilchi Suzuki, Naomi Taniguchi, Junzo Suzuki, and Teisuki Tanaka — along with three mechanics, a team manager, and a representative from American Honda Motor Company in Los Angeles. After mulling things over for a few moments, the agents let them through, even though the paperwork was all fake, a ruse used by Honda in Japan to get around travel restrictions in the home country. Because Honda didn't export motorcycles to Europe at the time and couldn't easily get exit visas, the men were listed as employees of an established trading company that did have business contacts overseas.

Honda had come to the United Kingdom for one reason only, to compete in the most important motorcycle road race on Earth, the Isle of Man TT. Traditionally a 37.73-mile race down narrow two-lane country roads, across ancient stone bridges, and past landmarks with names such as Ballacraine and Gooseneck and Greg-Ny-Baa, the TT was the premier stop on the Grand Prix circuit at the time. Win there and every motorcyclist in the world would know your name. Company founder Soichiro Honda had promised as far back as 1954 not only to enter the TT but also to conquer it. "Since I was a small child, one of my dreams has been to compete in motor vehicle races all over the world with a vehicle of my own making, and to win . . . ," he wrote to company employees on March 20, 1954. "I am filled with an abundant, unshakable confidence that I can win. The fighting spirit that is my nature will no longer allow me to continue turning away."[1]

It was not bravado, though the words were premature. Soichiro wanted to compete in the 250 cc class the following year, but it was not until 1959 that he could enter four machines in the 125 cc class. The factory had purchased an Italian 125 cc machine from perennial lightweight favourite Mondial to study prior to the race, mostly for its chassis and suspension design. The Mondial and other bikes in this category were typically single-cylinder models. Soichiro always understood that more cylinders and more valves meant higher engine speed and better breathing and sometimes even better reliability because of lower reciprocating mass per part. He ordered four twin-cylinder racers built especially for the competition. Yet the ultra-rare "eight-valve" cylinder heads designed for the bikes were not even ready when the race team arrived.

Every June the Isle of Man, nestled between Great Britain and Ireland in the northern Irish Sea, swells with tens of thousands of tourists, nearly doubling the island's population, which today stands at 70,000. Fans can buy a prized seat in the historic grandstand or stop almost anywhere along the course as the racers roar by in a series of both professional and amateur events. Island residents need only open the shutters to their stone cottages and stick their heads out of the windows, but not too far — they really can almost touch the insanely fast riders as they speed by.

The Japanese contingent was the first team to arrive on the island for that year's competition. Not only had none of the racers ever seen a European road course before, but they also had only limited experience with true road racing. There was the 12-mile "road course" that skirted the Asama volcano northwest of Tokyo, but the surface there was merely hard-packed and rolled ash, hardly a true road-racing compound. Honda finally built its own test track in 1958, but at 1,450 metres in length it was little more than a narrow drag strip that ran parallel to the Arakawa River — the course dead-ended at a wooden barricade. There were no curves, bends, or turns on the course, or even rises and falls. Any test machine had to be stopped before it could be turned around — the track was only five metres wide. Yet the little, scrappy, 125 cc machines would be racing on the winding, even more treacherous, 17.6-kilometre Clypse Course on the Isle of Man that year, complete with more than 70 turns and several sharp rises and precipitous descents.

The Japanese were confident — they wouldn't have come to the island otherwise — but the month began badly for the team once they actually rode their bikes hard. The Honda racing bikes broke down as if they were homemade garage specials, which, in a sense, they were. The Japanese-made tires lost their rubber blocks, chains stretched and rollers flew off, spark plugs lost their electrodes, and the pistons burned holes in themselves. The primitive bottom-link suspension, essentially a pivot at the bottom of the front forks similar to what Honda sold on its cheapest scooters, bottomed out repeatedly on the bumpier stretches of the

Clypse Course. Mechanics and racers alike spent all their free time rebuilding the machines.

"All of us, from the team leader on down, worked till late," recalled mechanic Shunji Hirota. "The way we saw it, it was easier working at night, when we didn't have spectators. Then it appeared in the newspaper that the Japanese were like mice in the attic. You could hear them scurrying around at night, it said."

Their diligence and investment — the effort cost Honda a reputed 10,000 pounds sterling, as much as a season's race budget for most European and British teams — paid off. Three of the new cylinder heads finally arrived by airfreight from Japan, and tires and spark plugs were replaced with English products. On June 3, 1959, the Japanese made history. Even though they did not win, or even score a podium finish, all four Japanese riders finished the race, including as high as sixth place, and Honda won the prestigious manufacturer's prize in its size category. Honda had achieved what it really wanted — recognition, even respect.

On the trip back home, customs officials in London and airline staff suddenly knew all about Honda, and major newspapers back in Japan carried word of the achievement. There was no more talk about mice in the attic, either, Shunji Hirota noted with pride.

The Honda Motor Company can trace its roots to a piston ring shop that Soichiro Honda opened with money borrowed from family and friends in 1937. He was so dedicated to success that he worked all his waking hours, every day, and slept in the shop at night; his wife would bring him meals from home so that he never had to leave. His piston rings broke at an alarming rate, however, and he was told to enrol in a local technical school before building more. He bristled at the suggestion — a ticket that would gain you admission to a movie theatre was more valuable than a diploma from a technical school, he argued — but he did consult a local university professor on what was going wrong. The professor interrogated him, examined his product, and then said the rings needed more silicone so they wouldn't be too brittle. Soichiro followed this advice and soon began supplying Toyota, but a fire and allied bombing during the war destroyed his small factory in Hamamatsu, a garage, really, like so many small Oriental businesses. Undaunted, Soichiro opened the Honda Technical Research Institute in 1946 designing and assembling full engines, not just piston rings, and in 1948 he purchased 500 military surplus generators that he adapted for use as bolt-on motors for bicycles. The following year he appointed former travelling salesman Takeo Fujisawa managing director of the fledgling firm and offered him a share of the company in exchange for the equivalent of a $7,500 investment. Soichiro then borrowed $3,800 elsewhere and soon began turning out his first, true production engine, a 50 cc two-stroke that powered a pressed steel frame motorcycle, a concept he adapted from several German designs. The machine worked so well that Soichiro dubbed it "the Dream" because that's what it was, the fulfillment of his dream to build a complete motorcycle. It was to be the first of several distinct Hondas to go by that name, and by the end of 1949 he had 70 employees churning out 100 machines a month.

Honda and Fujisawa were perfect complements to each other. Both men lacked degrees or much book learning, and each had come up the hard way in status-conscious Japan. Honda was the son of a bicycle repairman, and Fujisawa had dropped out of middle school as a youth to support his ailing father and struggling mother. One of Fujisawa's earliest jobs had been addressing envelopes and postcards by hand for pennies a day, though he later became successful as a steel salesman.

Soichiro Honda was the more conspicuous of the two, even a self-conscious individualist. Although he insisted that workers and foremen inside his factories wear white uniforms to challenge themselves to work cleanly and efficiently, he would go to a board meeting or meet with financiers while still dressed in a greasy jumpsuit. He may have been constructing an image, or perhaps he was rubbing it in — most large Japanese businesses of the era were run by descendants of the *zaibatsu*, almost an oligarchy of the monied and privileged classes there and far up the social ladder from himself. "The most important thing for me is me," he once said, a surprising, even heretical, remark to make in Japan.

Takeo Fujisawa was closer to the stereotypical Japanese businessman, at least in appearance. He wore Western-style suits and was formal in his demeanour. He had built his entire career as a salesman on keeping his word. Yet Fujisawa was no less an individualist than Soichiro — he recruited talent not by merely promising people they could be part of a great company, but also by convincing them that they could be great engineers and business leaders in their own right and that the Honda Motor Company would be great because of them.

If Soichiro is considered the visionary, it is Fujisawa who's often credited as the production and marketing genius behind the firm's worldwide success. For example, in 1952 Fujisawa terminated a lucrative contract to supply motors to a larger motorcycle company in Japan because he wanted Honda to sell only complete machines under its own name. Fujisawa was right — by 1958 Honda was the largest motorcycle manufacturer in Japan, with 285,000 annual sales, including its best-selling Super Cub, later known as the Honda 50 in the United States. The Super Cub featured a sewing-machine-smooth four-stroke motor and a step-through frame like a motor scooter but larger-diameter, spoked wheels, just like a small motorcycle. By the late 1950s, Honda's total output had surpassed that of the entire British motorcycle industry, which peaked at 187,000 units in 1954, although the British made much larger machines.

The 1959 Isle of Man TT team manager, Kiyoshi Kawashima, succeeded Soichiro Honda as president of the giant firm in 1973 and oversaw its greatest expansion in the automobile industry. He was the most traditionally Japanese of the company's leaders, the consummate team player. "The strength of the individual is limited," he argued. "When an organized team goes to work, however, it has enormous power and can accomplish amazing things."

This stereotypically Japanese position may sound antithetical to the surprising individualism that Honda and Fujisawa were preaching, but operationally everyone was on the same page.

The Honda Motor Company invested heavily in research and development. A July 1956 internal newsletter by Fujisawa called on Honda to emulate American practice, which he said always committed 3 percent of gross revenue into engineering design and prototype fabrication; the Japanese factory used that figure as a benchmark for many years.

Fujisawa and Honda also backed the opening of a fully independent R&D facility, incorporated as a separate entity from Honda Motor Company in July 1960. This was something Bert Hopwood wanted to do at the various British marques he worked at over the years and that BSA fully achieved at Umberslade Hall only in the late 1960s. Contrary to the stereotype of Japanese workers as conformist and unimaginative, Fujisawa introduced flexible work hours for his R&D team so that members could come in and work during spurts of creative energy, and the dress code was entirely relaxed. This was years before such practices emerged in the high-tech industry in California's Silicon Valley.

Some of the Honda Motor Company's capital over the years came from MITI, the Ministry of International Trade and Industry, a government agency established in 1949 to help the war-torn country rebuild its manufacturing base and earn foreign currency. Yet it was Honda and other developing Japanese companies that were really taking the risks. For example, Honda often invested in new machinery and factories before the order books were filled. To use a gambling term, they bet on the come, something the British motorcycle manufacturers typically were unwilling to do. If they bet wrong, they'd go out of business.

Motorcycle registrations in America remained stagnant at about 500,000 a year throughout the 1950s, with Canadian registrations steady at about 55,000 annually during the same period.[2] Cumulatively, this figure was less than half of the comparable numbers in the much smaller United Kingdom by the end of the decade, where registrations had continued to grow after the war. Nevertheless, Honda, like the British, coveted the American market most. The American Honda Motor Company, a wholly owned subsidiary, opened its doors in an old photo studio on West Pico Boulevard in Los Angeles in June 1959. The company needed approval from the Ministry of Finance just to send $250,000 out of the home country to establish its toehold in America, and three of the original executives rented an apartment for $80 a month with one bedroom — that became an office, and all slept on the floor to save costs. Nor were the bikes very good in the beginning — the Japanese quickly learned that Americans rode their bikes faster and harder than in Japan, which led to blown gaskets and clutch failures in particular. Honda could have fixed the bikes under warranty, but it did better than that. The company met its first, inevitable teething problem by recalling all its bikes, including ones not yet sold, and returned the machines to Japan for complete tear-downs. "We couldn't believe it," said Kiyoshi Kawashima. "We had great confidence in our product, and here our reputation in America was practically destroyed before we could get started. Mr. Honda gave us a guarantee that we had an international product, and right before our eyes our motorcycles were malfunctioning."

In spite of that initial stumble, Honda had established a toehold. The big breakthrough came with a new market segment Honda knew it had to create in the United States. This was the province of its proven 50 cc Super Cub. Beginning in 1962, these small bikes were featured in a series of national magazine and billboard ads in America that proclaimed "You meet the nicest people on a Honda." The company's market research had found that consumers had a negative reaction to motorcycles, so the word "motorcycle" never appeared in the ad campaign. "Honda" simply became a generic term for lightweight, step-through motorbikes, just like "Kleenex" became a generic term for facial tissue. Honda was on its way — the company even bought two 90-second TV ads on the 1964 Academy Awards show, which also helped it to reach a totally new audience for motorized two-wheel vehicles.

To upgrade its image even further, American Honda ordered

its corporate staff to dress in suits and ties and encouraged its dealers to create brighter, more inviting showrooms. The issue was not conformity but professionalism. Instead of selling motorcycles in the back of someone else's appliance store, for example, the Honda dealerships were modelled after the best appliance stores. Honda sold 40,000 motorcycles via 750 dealers in America in 1962, and there was no looking back.

Three-time Daytona 200 winner Dick Klamfoth was an early Honda franchisee in Columbus, Ohio. "Honda approached me at a race meet up in New Hampshire," he recalled. "They wanted me to be a dealer. They didn't have any dealers east of the Mississippi. When I took it, I became dealer number 74. I was the first dealer east of the Mississippi. That was when 'you meet the nicest people on a Honda.' You remember the ad with the girl on the back seat? There were billboards everywhere. That ad sold motorcycles."

Klamfoth was coveted because he still had a name in motorcycle circles. The fact that he was associated with the legendary Manx Norton and BSA Gold Star models didn't hurt. Yet he noted that Honda typically didn't want former motorcycle racers in its dealer network. At the first national dealer show he attended, Klamfoth says the majority of franchisees didn't even ride motorcycles themselves, let alone race them in their youth.

In 1960, the Japan Motorcycle Federation invited legendary racer Geoff Duke to give riding demonstrations in Japan. He quickly accepted, shipping one of his private Manx Nortons by boat ahead of time. When Duke arrived in Tokyo on April 14th, he was met at the airport by a large contingent and a giant banner proclaiming "Welcome Mr. Geoff Duke." Then he was ushered into a room where young women dressed in kimonos presented him with bouquets of flowers.

Over the next five weeks, Duke visited fans at motocross and road courses as well as several motorcycle factories and parts suppliers. The Yamaha and Suzuki plants were much larger and more modern than what he had seen back in England, he marvelled. He was particularly impressed by the NGK Spark Plug Company factory, which produced 50,000 spark plugs a day.

But the Honda factory was the real showstopper. "I was surprised to find that, contrary to other factories I had visited, almost all the technical 'bods' here spoke very good English," he remembered. "And I was in the middle of a conducted tour of the factory with a party of these people, when suddenly I was asked if I would like to meet Mr. Honda in person. I looked around, but the only other person I could see close by was a very non-VIP-looking, slightly built man in grey slacks, a white coat and a cap with a large peak, rather like that of a baseball player. But Mr. Honda it was."

By this time, the Honda Motor Company had built a new test track, incorporating a couple of S curves into the course, but Duke complained that it was still too short to get up to maximum speed on faster bikes. Honda asked him to test both the 125 cc twin and the new, 250 cc, four-cylinder Grand Prix racers then under development. It was not a matter of showing off so much as needing feedback from somebody who really knew all about international racing.

Duke's Manx Norton arrived late in Japan, then was embargoed by customs for several days. Duke was able to demonstrate it only once, and he wasn't sorry — the one track where he was able to run the bike was partly gravel, and he didn't dare get it up to full speed. Nevertheless, he learned as much from the Japanese as they learned from him. "On the plane home, I had some time to think and made certain notes which I thought might serve to stir some of our manufacturers out of their complacency," he wrote. "But alas, this was not to be."[3]

Edward Turner, who had first studied the American market in person in 1939, decided to visit Japan himself later that summer. Don Brown said Turner ordered him to gather every Japanese motorcycle he could get his hands on in a warehouse in Los Angeles so Turner could personally ride them during a stopover on his way to the Orient. The following are excerpts from Turner's report to the BSA board upon his return.

> As a result of the tremendous growth of the Japanese motorcycle industry, and the worldwide repercussions to our

industry, it was decided that I should pay a visit to Japan to see first-hand what is going on. . . .

Japan today is the largest manufacturer in the world of motorcycles, all of excellent quality. One company of this largest national producer of motorcycles produces more motorcycles than the whole of the British Industry put together, and this is only one of the 20 or more motorcycle companies in full operation. They are producing well over half a million motorcycles a year (against 140,000 British) of which Honda produces approaching a quarter of a million. . . .

I see the Japanese today combining the intense conscientious, thorough and meticulous attention to detail of the German with the very open-handed uninhibited approach to sales of the most blatant American sales corporation. . . .

The speed with which the Japanese motorcycle companies can produce new designs and properly tested and developed models is startling, and the very large scientific and technical staff maintained at the principal factories is, of course, out of all proportion to anything ever visualized in this country or, for that matter, in the United States. Honda alone, the largest company, has an establishment of 400 technicians engaged in styling new manufacturing techniques, new designs, new developments, new approaches. . . .

The Honda factory was everything that one could desire in an up-to-date manufacturing conception for motorcycles, and although nothing I saw was beyond our conception and ability to bring about in our factories, it should be borne in mind that we have not now, nor ever have had, the quantities of any one product that would justify these highly desirable methods being used. They had a large number of single purpose, specially designed machine tools which reduce labour for any large component, such as a crankcase, to an absolute minimum. All components, except the very small ones such as gear shafts and gears more conveniently transported in trays, were moving on conveyors throughout the factory. Every section for the small, medium and large motorcycles being made was geared to a time cycle, all assembly being on moving bands. . . . Engine and machine assembly was moving and all the components seemed to go together consistently and without difficulty, as indeed they had to in order to maintain the timed stations. . . .[4]

Parts of the report were defensive. For example, Turner argued that British riders would always prefer the bold, sporting feel of the larger British machines that he liked to design and build, and he defended himself against the persistent argument that product lines between the different brands at BSA should be consolidated. Turner said that the UK industry's fans both at home and abroad demanded a full line of distinct machines for each brand or there would be no reason to choose one over the other. He may have been right on the latter point. So-called "badge engineering," in which one merely slaps different nameplates on the same machine, rarely works.

Turner also complained that Anglo-Japanese trade agreements in force at the time were a one-way street; a series of lesser agreements was finalized in November 1962 as the Treaty of Commerce, Establishment, and Navigation between Japan and the United Kingdom. Industry leaders at the time howled, but Board of Trade president Reginald Maudling declared, "It is certainly not our policy to preserve uncompetitive industries as monuments to Britain's industrial past."[5]

Yet a University of Birmingham (England) study conducted years later, long after the dust and haze of the old industrial battles themselves, also condemned "the blind and often suicidal devotion of British governments and their officials to free trade (exemplified in the 1962 Anglo-Japanese trade agreement which failed to extend to motorcycles, even temporarily, the quotas and voluntary controls put on imports of textiles, radios, etc. despite the lobbying of the British Motor Cycle Industries Association)."[6]

In contrast, the Italians steadfastly held on to substantial import quotas, which protected their important scooter manufacturers as well as motorcycle producers Ducati, MV Augusta, and Moto Guzzi, marques that survive to this day.

Recriminations are rife as to who is to blame for the demise of the British motorcycle industry, and Turner often has a big bull's eye painted on his forehead. Yet he understood the dilemma that British manufacturers faced well enough, even if his engineering skills were weak and his management style imperial. For example, a 1975 report by the Boston Consulting Group (BCG) supported Turner's contention that Japan's huge home market justified the investment in expensive, custom-made, single-purpose machine tools but that Great Britain's home market did not justify the same kind of commitment.

Having that home market proved to be a huge advantage, even if profit margins per unit were tiny. What the Japanese gained from producing all those smaller machines was knowledge they employed in making larger machines for export both better and more cost effective. The BCG called this the *price experience curve*. "Each time the accumulated experience of manufacturing a particular product doubles, the total unit cost in real terms . . . can be made to decline by a characteristic percentage, normally in the region of 20 to 30 percent," the report concluded.[7]

The Japanese did not enter the American and British markets late in the game, as some think, but with a considerable head start. The idea that they had to play catch-up with the West, or overtake Western manufacturers, is misleading.

Not all analyses employed the theoretical constructions and mathematical models favoured by the BCG, however. Richard T. Pascale rather more simply, even ironically, said that Honda's American success was due to the Japanese company's "miscalculation, serendipity and organizational learning" as well as the "idiosyncratic characters and leadership of company founders Soichiro Honda and Takeo Fujisawa, the product design (rather than production process, pointedly) advantages that Honda developed, in particular the wedding of a high-tech small engine to an innovative design in the 1958 Super Cub small motorcycle."[8] Put another way, Pascale argued that Honda had no grand strategy — Honda succeeded in conquering the world because it didn't know it couldn't be done and because it made a superior product that people found irresistible.

Back in England a few months after Turner's 1960 visit to Japan, a small group of warehousemen surrounded several crates of Made-in-Japan motorcycles at the BSA factory loading dock in Small Heath. Peter Glover, who retired as export market manager for BSA in 1973, was there too. "We had three or four crates from Japan, and I was in a position to say these are not intended for us, but let's have a look anyway," he recalled. "We pried open the crates, and they were all Japanese motorcycles. Edward Turner had ordered them. We had never seen anything like them," said Glover, who recalled a 250 cc parallel twin Honda Dream model with a pressed steel frame but also mid-sized bikes from other manufacturers, including a smallish v-twin from an unknown company. "I sent the machines up to the experimental department, and they were looked at by the technical director at the time. He had a close look at these bikes, particularly the Honda, and there was something to do in the valve gear. He said [that] to purchase the plant to produce that component would take the whole of [his] machine tool budget for the year. I don't remember what the component was."

Still, the mood in Birmingham was one of official optimism. BSA published a special company newsletter on June 7, 1961 — the 100th anniversary of the formation of the company — and touted its 3-million-pound profit for the previous year. Jack Sangster, the wheeler-dealer who built his personal fortune by acquisitions and mergers, also announced his retirement as chairman of the company in the newsletter, though he retained a seat on the board, a position that still had some merit in those days. In the first chair, though, he was succeeded by Eric Turner (no relation to Edward), lately of the British aeronautics industry. "Eric Turner was the youngest colonel in the British army in the Second World War," noted Keith Blair, a former BSA management trainee and later executive with Norton Villiers Triumph. "He emerged from the army and had what we called a good war. He was a wonderful-looking man, very smart, immaculate hair. He was the sort of person who would show up in a car at the BSA factory, and someone would clip a carnation on his lapel. Then he would go off for a couple of hours and say, 'Very well, good show, carry on,' and get back in his car."

Eric Turner also turned to the McKinsey Consulting Company to recommend improvements to the automotive group within BSA, a step that outraged long-time company managers. It was "McKinseys," as the company was casually known, that famously called motorcycles "consumer durables." The consultants recommended that production between BSA, Triumph, and Ariel be consolidated (badge engineering), a policy that went far beyond the mere sharing of relatively nondescript parts such as brakes or shock absorbers. McKinsey also warned that sales in America would peak unless more contemporary machines were offered — about this the company was quite prescient.[9]

The major British manufacturers have been called complacent, even smug, for their lack of forward thinking in the decades after World War II, but it's not quite true. It would be more correct to say that management made poor choices when they were flush with money. Triumph, which should have known better, lost heavily with the Tigress and Tina. BSA further shot itself in the foot when it introduced the 75 cc Beagle and the somewhat similar 50 cc Ariel Pixie in late 1962. Both had large-diameter, wire-spoke wheels and four-stroke motors, which helped to distinguish them from the Italian scooter marque, and which were quite similar to the little Hondas in these aspects. Unlike the BSA offerings, however, the competing Honda retained the traditional scooter "step-through" frame design, which proved to be the right combination for this end of the market. Alas, neither the Beagle nor the Pixie was successful, and each was withdrawn within three years after enjoying very limited sales, representing a serious financial hit for the parent firm.

Both marques also introduced "new," large-capacity models in the early 1960s. One long-standing criticism of all large English motorcycles referred to their separate engines and gearboxes, the two components being connected by a primary chain. It all looked rather untidy and old-fashioned and forced designers to make frames a bit longer than they otherwise would have preferred. BSA had introduced a 250 cc "unit construction" model, with the engine and transmission built "in unit," in 1959, while Triumph had introduced a 350 cc unit twin a few years before that. Yet it wasn't until 1962 and 1963, respectively, that BSA and Triumph converted their flagship 650 cc bikes to unit construction. These were the heavily chromed BSA Lightning, Thunderbolt, and Spitfire models as well as the far subtler, always delightfully coloured Triumph Bonneville and Trophy models.

These lusty machines remained little changed in other regards, however. Braking continued to be deficient, especially at the increasingly higher speeds the bikes could attain; some still had primitive six-volt electrics and very poor lights; and none of the new unit construction models had electric starting. The British also retained separate oil tanks for lubrication. While this had certain advantages in high-performance motors, it created messy external oil lines. Both Honda and Ducati were already employing "wet sump" engine design, meaning the oil supply was carried at the bottom of the engine itself, as in automobile practice.

Worse, the British continued to use vertically split crankcases that invariably leaked oil from the seam that ran along the bottom of the engines. This is why British motorcycle retailers often put small pie pans under their machines to catch oil that otherwise would drip onto the showroom floor. It was the vertical split that mandated a separate tank to carry the oil, and it was the refusal of the British to invest in pressure die-casting equipment that forced them to build up their crankcases from vertically split halves.

Performance *was* raised in the new unit construction models, typically by playing with the valve gear and boosting engine compression. Even this represented a dubious achievement, as such tuning tricks were better left to the after-market and back-street performance shops. Higher compression in particular led to overheating, increased jack hammer-like engine vibration, and reduced reliability. Nevertheless, the bikes looked good and went well, and in 1966 both Triumph and BSA were presented with the Queen's Award to Industry for achievement in exports. Each company was exporting about 75 percent of its products at the time, mostly to the United States.[10]

Bert Hopwood, who left Norton for a second time in 1961 to rejoin Triumph, no longer believed in Edward Turner's parallel twin engine design. He had become an apostle of modular engine design in which many of the same parts from individual cylinders — pistons, connecting rods, valve springs, and so on — could be shared in engines using multiples of the same basic cylinder. Yet designing such a motor from scratch proved unrealistic in England at the time, so Hopwood and his chief engineering aide, Doug Hele, did some initial work on a three-cylinder 750 cc engine based on the existing twin-cylinder Triumph 500 cc. The same pistons, connecting rods, and so on would be used in each cylinder, but a new crankcase would have to be developed for the wider engine, of course.

"Doug Hele had been nagging me for years to give consideration to a three-cylinder engine design for larger capacity units," Hopwood wrote. "One evening late in 1963, after everyone had gone home, we sat in his office [and] to amuse ourselves we laid out the basic outline of what later became the 750 cc Trident."[11]

Again, just as Joe Craig had discovered years earlier when he and John Surtees had approached Edward Turner about building a four-cylinder racer at Triumph, the triple concept was also rejected by Turner. He thought the bike would be too costly to put in production, would be too heavy, and would be rejected by the Americans because it had an odd number of cylinders.

Norton was having its own problems by the late 1950s. The single-cylinder works racers were no longer built after the mid-1950s, though a limited number of replica bikes with parts support continued in production for several years more. In spite of being rooted in the 1920s, these Manx Nortons had remained competitive against the much more modern, overhead cam "fours" from Gilera and MV Augusta, at least through the early 1950s, only because they benefited from 30 years of development, while the Italian jobs were still new and had teething problems. But the Italians — and later the Japanese, who copied them — were right. The transverse-mounted, overhead cam, multi-valve "fours" were the dominant high-performance engines well into the twenty-first century. When Norton abandoned its own half-hearted, underfunded, four-cylinder effort with partner BRM in 1952, it was all over in the comp shop.

The business side wasn't doing much better. Since 1951, Norton had been part of conglomerate AMC — Associated Motor Cycles — that traced its roots to brothers Harry and Charlie Collier, racers in the early Isle of Man TT who also founded Matchless in London. Over the years, the company came to acquire the AJS, James, and Francis-Barnett marques and ultimately Norton. Not unlike BSA management, AMC kept its two leading brands, Matchless and Norton, quite separate. Matchless bikes were produced at Woolwich, a London suburb on the south bank of the Thames, while Norton remained holed up in the Bracebridge Street factory in Birmingham suburb Aston. Hopwood, who had returned to Norton in 1956 in the never-ending merry-go-round that was the British motorcycle industry, wanted a newer factory. The technology was so antiquated that many of the lathes were still operated by leather belts.

Finally, in 1961, Hopwood made a verbal agreement to buy a vacant factory in the same Aston suburb where the Norton plant was situated. This was important to him, he said, as most of the skilled factory workers lived nearby and would not be put out by the change. The price was set at 250,000 pounds sterling, and just as he was about to cut the cheque he was ordered by his bosses to forward the "factory money" to London. Hopwood was infuriated, and this was his stated reason for leaving the brand a second time in 1961. But AMC really did need the money.

The Matchless street bikes weren't selling well. In particular, its own 650 cc twin motors proved unreliable when tuned for higher performance in an effort to remain competitive in the marketplace. AMC had begun some parts consolidation between brands in the late 1950s when Matchless began supplying its well-regarded transmissions to Norton, and in the 1960s Norton began supplying complete engines to Matchless for its 650 cc and 750 cc models. Finally, in 1962 AMC closed the historic Norton factory for good, moving all production to London. It guaranteed only one employee a job — the factory storesman, who could identify every Norton part by sight.[12]

Technically speaking, closing the old Norton factory was no great loss — a contemporary observer called the factory "a rabbit warren," and another had labelled the whole site "a Victorian slum." Nevertheless, one pundit at the time said, "It's almost as unthinkable as if Nelson were to desert his column."[13]

The first new Norton to be built at Woolwich was the 400 cc Electra. As its name suggests, it had electric starting, and the Berliner brothers placed a large order for these and other Norton machines in January 1963. Nevertheless, AMC continued to lose money and was in debt to the tune of 1.5 million pounds by 1965. By the following year, that figure had jumped to 2.2 million pounds. Adjusted for devaluation and inflation, these sums would be at least 10 times the original figures today.[14]

AMC went into receivership in 1966 and in September of that year was effectively merged with Villiers, a company that supplied most of the two-stroke engines used in various small British motorcycles as well as lawn mowers, cultivators, and the like — it was truly the Briggs & Stratton of England. Villiers had only recently been absorbed itself by Manganese Bronze Holdings (MBH), a company best known for making ships' propellers. In short order, a new entity was formed called Norton Villiers, which ultimately reported to Manganese Bronze's chairman, former amateur race car driver Dennis Poore. Alas, the Matchless line was put down, along with lesser marques James and Francis-Barnett.

On the racing front, British riders continued to do well, though no longer on British bikes. Phil Read won seven world championships for Yamaha and MV Augusta, and Jim Redman, a controversial rider who left England and moved to Rhodesia at age 17 in part to avoid military conscription, won six world championships for Honda. Redman also repeatedly and publicly complained about the lack of rider safety on the Grand Prix circuit yet was so trusted by Honda that he was race team captain and manager for much of the 1960s. But it was Mike Hailwood — "Mike the Bike" the motorcycling press liked to call him — who was to be the most famous motorcycle racer of the 1960s and '70s, both for his victories and for his wild and woolly riding style. Riding for Honda in 1961, he won both the 125 cc and the 250 cc classes in the Isle of Man TT, only two years after the Japanese giant had arrived on the island. What's more, he won the FIM-sanctioned world championship in the 250 cc class that year.

Hailwood's early career in England proved to be controversial. Mike was talented but privileged too. His father, Stan, was a successful motorcycle dealer who spared no expense in getting the best bikes for his son early on in his career. The Hailwood "equipe," as the British always liked to style their more organized teams, was the best funded of all privateers on the British Isles. Mike Hailwood was a very good young racer, yet successful period racer Derek Minter once alleged that Stan offered him money to stay out of a race that Mike had entered, presumably to increase the boy's chances of winning. Another time Stan allegedly ordered a gaggle of motorcycle journalists to tout his son's recent performance or else he'd withhold advertising from their magazines.[15] It's true the pushy yet insecure James Vincent Smith had helped his son, Jeff, get a head start in Observed Trials and motocross, and Jack Surtees, who owned a Vincent dealership, often travelled with his son, John, but Stan was almost like the Godfather.

The analogy is not misguided. Stan Hailwood left school when he was 13 to work in a wagon factory. At 16, he began buying and selling used motorcycles, often rebuilding wrecks and cashing in on them. When he was 21, he joined the Howard King "motorcycle emporium" in Oxford as a mechanic, but because he walked with a limp he was paid only on commission. A great salesman, he played hardball at the wholesale level, demanding major concessions in return for his trade, and at retail he was the consummate gladhander, able to convince customers he was giving them the best price possible just because he liked them. He also pioneered easy credit for young men who wanted to purchase his machines, and he would personally call on them to collect a debt if need be. In time, Stan acquired King's, opening

21 dealerships in the United Kingdom and selling up to 12,000 machines a year.

John Surtees was to express sympathy for his young rival, Mike Hailwood, specifically on account of his father. "I remember feeling sorry for Mike, because if ever anybody set out to manufacture a world champion, Stan set out to make Mike one, and fed him relentlessly into a starmaking machine fuelled by his money and his overwhelming personality."[16]

If Mike was pushed into the limelight by his dad, he earned the right to bask in it all by himself. An honest competitor who once complained that other riders tried to win by blocking rather than trying to go faster themselves, he won nine Grand Prix road-racing titles between that first one in 1961 and 1967, riding for both MV Augusta and Honda. He also won an astonishing 14 Isle of Man TT races in various size categories. Yet Hailwood was considered a sloppy rider — put his knee out too far, slid around on his seat too much, bobbed his head a lot. Yet he won. He was especially fast and fearless in the corners, which is where you'd make up distance on bikes that were as fast or faster than yours. Put another way, he leaned over as far or farther than anyone else in his right mind would. "If you don't fall off occasionally, you are not trying hard," he famously said throughout his career.

It was only in scrambles that a British manufacturer — BSA — slogged on relentlessly, placing all bets on its star off-road rider Jeff Smith. Smith had won many British titles and individual Grand Prix motocross events, but year after year he came up short of the world championship.

After the 1959 riding season, Smith switched from the Gold Star to a machine based on BSA's smaller commuter bike, the single-cylinder 250 cc C15, which factory engineers were now improving and enlarging. The basic bike had proven successful and reliable when enlarged to 350 cc, so much so that the British army became a major customer. Yet even though it was Smith himself who argued for a new, lighter dirt bike, he was surprised one day by results of a side-by-side test that new comp shop manager Brian Martin had arranged between the "Goldie" and what ultimately became the Victor model. Jeff rode the Gold Star over a prescribed course; then he switched to the smaller, 350 cc machine for another go at it. The "350" felt like it had the slower time, Jeff said after the test. He was chagrined and conceded that he must have been wrong in wanting a lighter machine. He promised he'd stick with the Gold Star after all. But Martin pulled out a slip of paper on which he had recorded stopwatch times for both bikes — the Victor had been several seconds faster around the course.

A production Gold Star weighed about 340 pounds. A full-on dirt racer version cut that number by 50 pounds — strip the lighting, substitute alloy fenders, drill holes in the rear brake's torque arm to lose an ounce here, an ounce there. But the 350 cc Victor in racing trim got down to 228 pounds. The smaller Victor motor also gave away several horsepower, so it was a wash at first. Jeff campaigned the bike for the next several years and did well, but still he failed to score a world championship. By the spring of 1964, in what would be his 30th year, the motorcycling press had written him off. A cache of Swedish riders continued to dominate on the continent in motocross, including Rolf Tibblin, the 1962 and '63 champ on his Swedish-built Husqvarna. Smith decided that 1964 would be his year of decision — he'd win, or he'd pack it in. In the winter of 1963–64, he trained particularly hard with fellow BSA employee Maurice Herriott, a man who trained so hard he always looked sick yet who went on to win the silver medal in the 3,000-metre steeplechase event at the 1964 Tokyo Olympics. Herriott and Smith would run past the row houses and through the nearby neighbourhoods at Small Heath and up a long hill in the field across from the factory. Sometimes other lads from the factory would join them on their daily 45-minute runs; Smith says he was always happy when they'd fall by the wayside, maybe bend over, and puke. He might be beat, but he wouldn't quit.

Smith's preseason began with his unofficial championship in the amazingly popular BBC Grandstand series, which broadcast motocross races to audiences in the foulest weather in the depth of winter every Saturday afternoon. The live television broadcasts from venues in England and Wales drew a huge following, including among the non-motorcycling public. Rules were flexible there — no restarts, and lax enforcement on the track, too, though no one really tried to crash out competitors in what were, after all, non-championship events. One of the main reasons BSA continued funding Smith's increasingly expensive motocross exploits was because of all the free publicity he garnered by dominating this series.

The real Grand Prix season for 1964 started in earnest in Switzerland that spring. It had rained the day before the meet, which isn't always a bad thing. "The ground can be very trustworthy," said Smith. "There's a moment when the track is absolutely perfect, but that usually lasts only five or six laps." He was second in the event to Swedish rider Rolf Tibblin. As standard now, Smith rode his Victor, which had been punched out further to 420 cc. Yet Smith was to finish second in the next three races as well. Another championship appeared to be slipping away.

Smith finally won in his fifth start of the season, at the Dutch Grand Prix, and he stayed close to the top throughout the rest of the season. The final race was in Spain in September, and Tibblin and Smith were tied with 54 points each. Whoever won there would win the world championship. "We went to Spain five days early," said Smith. "The track was on a golf course, which was a beautiful place to put a motocross course, though it didn't please the golfers. We walked the course every day after noon, which was the hottest portion of the day so we'd get used to the heat."

The race proved to be anti-climactic. Tibblin crashed on the third lap, and Smith just had to finish to win. "It was tremendous," he said. "The prize presentation was not on blocks, here's first place, here's second place. The finish was in a sand quarry, so we went up to a cliff and stood on it. There were a great number of fans about. They hung a laurel wreath around me and presented me with two trophies, one for winning the event and the other for the championship. I remember looking out at the sea of faces and being somewhat emotionally affected. Here I was, after all these years, and I was a world champion."

Chapter Six

Industrial Action

BRIGHT LIGHTS AND A BIG-CITY exhibition hall — this was Earls Court in late 1967. The annual London motorcycle show was still the most important in the world, even if the British motorcycle industry no longer was. Most of the marques on display were European — from Bultaco to CZ — or Japanese. Yet BSA and Triumph each had recently won a queen's award for outstanding performance in exports and were well represented at the show. The new Norton Villiers Company, recently established by Dennis Poore from the picked-over remains of Associated Motor Cycles, also debuted a sensational new model, the Commando. This was a medium-weight motorcycle with a sturdy 750 cc engine fitted to a new frame that virtually eliminated the jack hammer vibration British twins were known for and dressed with a slick fibreglass gas tank and "fastback" tail section alongside narrow, sporty chromed fenders. It looked fast, and it was fast. Best of all, it was British.

Like some other bikes at the show, the Norton Commando stood on a small turntable with spotlights reflected in the chrome and shiny paint as gangly young men with greasy hair and duck tail curls, all looking like young ton-up boys, squeezed close to gam a look-see. "The public was stunned by its stark modernity," wrote one magazine retrospective.[1]

Poore was beaming. Nothing succeeds like success. Yet the Norton Commando had barely existed on paper three months earlier, and it wasn't supposed to exist at all. What Poore really wanted when he bought out AMC in 1966 was to introduce a truly new double overhead cam, unit construction, 800 cc machine under development by Dr. Stefan Bauer, recently of Rolls-Royce. That new engine was plagued with failures on the test bench, and it vibrated as much as other twins; worse, it produced no more power than the tried-and-true pushrod twin long in use by the company.

What to do? Late in the summer of 1967, a decision was made to chuck the "800" and fit the older engine into a new frame that would look good and take care of vibration by other means. This was the Commando, and it featured a unique, rubber-mounted subframe that isolated the entire engine and transmission to reduce vibration. Previous attempts at rubber mounting had merely placed rubber washers on the bolts that fastened an engine to a frame. Norton's innovation, mostly credited to Bauer's assistants Bernard Hooper and Bob Trigg, was dubbed "Isolastic," and it was true — most of the terrible engine vibration was isolated from rider contact points such as the footpegs and handlebars, but the frame could be quite elastic as the rubber bushings wore over time. The bike was introduced at a reasonable price in April 1968 and proved a hit, especially in America.

The Commando was voted bike of the year by readers of an important British motorcycle magazine five years in a row, and Brian Slark, a former service manager for Norton Villiers in Long Beach, California, said Americans drooled over the machine once they discovered it. "For such a little company, we got on the cover of *Cycle* and *Cycle World*," he said. "We would show up at the dealers on the motorcycle. We would encourage the dealer to come out and ride the bikes with us. We just appealed to their enthusiasm. Within a short while, we sold 1,000 motorcycles and went from there."

Poore also unveiled a new marketing scheme at Norton Villiers. Instead of emphasizing its racing heritage, the company promoted a series of ads featuring buxom women with partly unbuttoned blouses, thigh-high miniskirts, and vinyl go-go boots, often sitting suggestively on the bikes. The ads were so successful the models came to be known as "the Norton girls," and reprints are widely available on the Internet to this day. The company sold 10,000 Commandos worldwide in each of 1968 and 1969.[2]

Commando production was soon moved from Woolwich, just outside London, out of necessity — the premises, which were wanted for a housing estate, had become the subject of a Greater London Council compulsory purchase order, equivalent to a claim of eminent domain, in late 1968. Most of the heavy line work was transferred to Wolverhampton, where Villiers two-stroke engines had long been made, and a new, smaller design studio plus a final assembly plant were built at Andover, near the old Thruxton air field in southwestern England. Still, the bikes were well received, and sales continued to improve. Soon Dennis Poore was proclaimed a hero. It was he who had saved Norton, one of the crown jewels of British manufacturing history.

Roger Dennistoun "Dennis" Poore was born in Paddington, London, in 1916, just before his father was killed in World War I. The Poores came from wealthy Scottish stock, and Dennis was educated at Eton and Cambridge. Later he became Chairman and ultimately obtained controlling interest in a company called Manganese Bronze, which supplied ships' propellers in that alloy to Cunard and other luxury liner companies. A dashing man about town, he raced a small MG sports car before World War II, then rose to the rank of wing commander in the Royal Air Force during the war, stationed at Thruxton. After the conflict, he hauled an Alfa-Romeo sports car behind a Ford V-8 truck, then a Dodge pick-up, to race meets all over the country. The trucks were a sight on English roads — both had left-hand drive. Poore wasn't a bad racer, and he drove briefly for the Connaught team on the international Grand Prix circuit, finishing as high as 4th in the British Grand Prix and 12th in the Italian Grand Prix in 1952. "He was just a very educated, well-spoken man, very bright with figures," recalled Slark. "He was a city gent. He had his office at 1 Love Lane in the shadow of St. Paul's Cathedral. He was a very typical, well-spoken British businessman, very well dressed."

Mike Jackson, who was general manager at Norton Villiers Corporation in the 1970s, also recalls Poore positively. "My first meeting with Poore was at the [1969] 250 Dutch motocross Grand Prix. AJS [a brand Norton Villiers owned] were contesting the World Championship that year, so, subject to location, he would fly over on the morning of the race. He liked, approved, and understood the 'race on Sunday/sell on Monday' racing philosophy. In answer to his question about what I thought of that year's AJS effort, I boldly stated that I thought we were slightly out of our depth in this series, inasmuch as, instead of our riders ending up the year in, say, fifth or eighth place in the World Championship, we'd be better off competing in the British championship and winning that. He fixed me with a laser gaze, which was scary, whereupon his features softened, saying, 'Given the comparative costs, I think you may be right.'"

Yet it was his boardroom machinations that were to stamp Poore, rightly or wrongly, as an opportunist, even a predator. For example, moving Commando final assembly to Andover was controversial given that he had capacity elsewhere and workers who wanted to keep their jobs — critics said he did it only to qualify for tax-supported government incentives. And the closure of the former Matchless factory at Woolwich was almost as lamented in the press as the Norton factory closure in Birmingham by AMC several years earlier. "I went back to AMC in 1969, and they were taking the machinery out," recalled Slark. "There were boards hanging down and power cords hanging down. It was just an old, empty shell. There had been fathers and sons who had worked there together. It was just very, very sad. There's not even a street named for the factory to signify it was ever there."

BSA and Triumph also brought new "superbikes" to market in 1968 — they were the BSA Rocket 3 and Triumph Trident, both of which featured nearly identical three-cylinder 750 cc motors. They were based on Bert Hopwood and Doug Hele's earlier idea of taking a 500 cc twin Triumph motor and plunking a similar cylinder in the middle. Harry Sturgeon, who succeeded Edward Turner as head of BSA and Triumph motorcycle divisions in 1964, was so enthusiastic about the triple when he heard about it at a board meeting that he ordered Hopwood to start on a prototype right away, without the need to even show him technical drawings first.

Sturgeon was a controversial choice to replace the ailing Edward Turner, who was suffering from type II diabetes. One report says he came from the Havilland Aircraft Company; others say he had been promoted from recently acquired BSA subsidiary Churchill Grinding Machine Company. Either way he hadn't come up through the motorcycle ranks, and that was resented. Worse, he never moved to Birmingham, preferring to stay on his farm out in Hertfordshire when he wasn't tending to company business. When he did appear in Birmingham, he stayed in a hotel. Hopwood in particular was indignant that he had been passed over for the top motorcycle job, but many associates had long been ambivalent about his managerial capabilities, noting his unwillingness to actually command people and then to complain about events after the fact. He had his backers, of course. Wilf Harrison, a former service manager at BSA, was sent to America in 1964 or '65 to meet with dealers who were struggling with warranty claims against the big twins, especially electrical problems. When he returned to England, he met with Hopwood and several other engineers in what was to become a ritual after several more trips to dealers in the United States. "After decisions were made, [Hopwood] would turn to me and ask if I was happy," Harrison recalled. "If I said I was, he would say, 'Very well, that's decided then.' But if I said I wasn't happy, he'd say, 'Well, we can't send him back to America,' and we'd continue to work on the problem."

But others looked down on his management style. At one

meeting during the early 1960s in Meriden chaired by Edward Turner, several designs were being bandied about by various people, yet Hopwood didn't speak up once, even though he was Triumph managing director at the time. Frustrated, Turner turned to him, bellowing that he should "Say something, Hopwood, even if it's only a grunt."[3]

The smartly dressed Sturgeon may not have been a motorcycle man, but he was considered a marketing genius of sorts. He approved, for example, a new series of expensive, full-colour print motorcycle ads that featured casually dressed, attractive young men and women on or near shining motorcycles in sunny locales such as a Santa Monica harbour. Helmets were never included in the ads, and in fact the models didn't even "ride" the motorcycles. It was more of a lifestyle presentation, an advance on Honda's "nicest people" theme. Such prospective buyers also represented, not coincidentally, the first wave of the baby boom generation in England and America as it turned 18. Motorcycle division revenues shot up 40 percent between 1964 and 1966 at BSA Group, quite in line with what was happening in the sporty automobile market too.

Sturgeon kept the factories humming too. "[Sturgeon] moved the industry from being one based on craft volume to an industry based on production volumes," said Keith Blair. "It was his idea to get production up. 'It's ridiculous to say we've got 18 weeks of production sold and that's it,' he would say."[4]

He also abhorred haggling with labour and once stepped in to a particularly tense set of contract talks in Birmingham, offering the workers *more* than they were demanding — he hadn't bothered to study previous minutes from his negotiating team.[5]

Sturgeon liked the "race on Sunday/sell on Monday" approach — that's why factory racers returned to Daytona in the mid-1960s, albeit mounted on Triumphs. But his most important decision was to "green light" the triples. The actual development work is usually credited to Doug Hele.

Like so many leaders in the British motorcycle industry, Hele was both a Birmingham native (born in 1919) and a man without a four-year university pedigree. He had been apprenticed to the Austin car company before the war, moving to the Douglas motorcycle company after hostilities ceased. An expert in both engine and chassis design, he once complained to his superiors at Douglas that their flagship "opposed twin" didn't handle well, and he offered to lend his personal BSA motorcycle to boss George Halliday so he could see how a proper bike went. Hele was promptly fired for his impertinence.[6]

Hele encouraged dissent by his staff and once said that an hour gabbing over different designs at lunch was worth more than a formal written proposal with detailed engineering plans. His modesty was proven when, after catching a lift with a friend to attend the funeral of an important motorcycle industry executive, he insisted on paying for gas. Another time, while working at Norton, Hele was in his office so late at night that his wife called the police to see what the matter was. An investigating policeman couldn't get into the plant, so he threw stones at the only lighted window he saw. Hele had to be convinced to go home.

He personally tuned the Triumph 500 cc twins that won the Daytona 200-mile race in 1966 and 1967 with American riders Buddy Elmore and Gary Nixon aboard respectively. He said he'd send race bikes to America only at the last minute because American tuners "would lose 2 brake horsepower per week" if they got their paws on the machines first. Nevertheless, he was highly regarded by Americans whom he worked with when he did visit the United States.[7]

Initial styling of the 1968 triples was problematic — the gas tank, the most visual element of a motorcycle after the engine — was squarish, even "truck-like," according to one contemporary critic. Additionally, the BSA version was mocked for its conspicuous "ray gun" mufflers. Both features were quickly abandoned, and the bikes were moderately successful during their production run. The engines made 58 horsepower in stock form and could achieve an honest 118 mph, excellent specifications for the day. Plus, the model proved successful on the racetrack. In 1971, the BSA Group entered a brace of three-cylinder bikes under both the Triumph and the BSA names at the annual Daytona 200. Top rider Mike Hailwood was given the fastest BSA, and future legend Paul

Smart, another Englishman, was given the best Triumph. To cover its bets, BSA also hired American ace Dick Mann to pilot a Rocket 3. Mann had won in 1970 on a Honda 750, and he won again in 1971. It was to be the last time a British bike would win the prestigious event. The triples also did well under the Triumph brand for several years in production racing events at the Isle of Man, particularly with a popular race-prepped version nick-named by the press "Slippery Sam."

The impetus to bring the Commando and BSA/Triumph triples to market in 1968 came from the Orient. Honda had introduced a 450 cc, double overhead cam, four-stroke bike in 1965 that was almost equal in performance to the English big twins but sized a little too small for the marketplace. It was oddly styled as well — its nickname was the "Black Bomber" because of its very black, very bulbous (even camel-like) gas tank with gratuitous chrome panels and a black tubular frame with matte grey fenders. Also pouring in from the Orient by the mid-1960s were vastly improved 250 cc and 350 cc two-stroke road machines from Suzuki, Yamaha, Kawasaki, and Bridgestone, some of which were already *faster* than the British four-strokes. There had always been resistance to two-strokes for the street because they burned oil by design and because of their sputtering, pop-corn-machine exhaust note. Yet one great innovation from Japan was automatic oil injection — no longer did two-stroke owners have to carefully measure out oil and mix it with the gasoline themselves.

The British had a gun to their heads. The bullet in the last chamber? A rumoured large-capacity, four-cylinder Honda. The British beat that bike to market by a year, but it didn't help them much. In 1969, Honda introduced its legendary CB750, a 750 cc model with features no one could touch — four cylinders, single overhead cam, electric starting, and front disc brake. It even had four exhaust pipes and mufflers, just to make sure customers understood something different was happening here. The bike was rated at 67 horsepower; top speed was 123 mph. It had a five-speed transmission and sold for $1,495 in the United States. More than 400,000 of the bikes were sold during its nine-year production run.

"For those who didn't personally experience the revolution that Honda launched with the 1969 CB750, it's difficult to fully comprehend the impact of this landmark motorcycle," a 2004 Honda press release quite accurately touted. "In 1969 Honda had been in America for only 10 years, and at that time European bikes — especially British — defined the parameters of high performance. In one deft move, Honda instantly elevated the entire motorcycle industry to a new and higher plane. Suddenly, the heretofore contradictory elements of jaw-dropping performance, engineering sophistication and mechanical reliability would become interwoven into a seamless whole, thanks to the CB750."[8]

The British bikes were found wanting in comparison. The sun was eclipsing the moon. Indeed, neither the Commando nor the triples were truly new — far from it. Besides old motors, or old motor parts in the case of the semi-modular triples, the bikes had four-speed transmissions, drum brakes, and kick-starting. The British should have been scared, very scared.

They were. Although Poore killed off the new but reluctant 800 cc motor in development when he bought Norton in 1966, he told colleagues he intended to build a true world beater in time, and he meant it. In 1971, the company entered a partnership with famed Formula 1 race car engine builder Cosworth to design a water-cooled, double overhead cam, 750 cc machine. The Cosworth Challenge engine, as it was called, was rated at an optimistic 110 horsepower in racing tune, but even if the actual figure was significantly less the motor would have been a sensation had it only worked. It didn't, and the project was dropped in 1975 — the third failure in a line of failures going back to the BRM "four" Geoff Duke had wanted in the early 1950s.

The BSA Group made a more significant effort to stem the Japanese tide. Harry Sturgeon died of a brain tumour in 1966, and Hopwood, who had been acting engineering director of the motorcycle division during the man's waning months, was passed over yet again for the permanent appointment, this time in favour of a complete outsider, Lionel Jofeh, a former Sperry Gyroscope Company managing director. Hopwood quickly resigned; his resignation was refused; he stayed on. People were learning how to handle him.

"Jofeh wasn't a big man. His background was in engineering," recalled Wilf Harrison. "He knew nothing about motorbikes. He didn't even like them."

Harrison did like motorcycles and regularly commuted between the Triumph factory in Meriden and the BSA plant in Small Heath on two wheels. Yet when he showed up for a business lunch at the BSA executive dining hall one day in full leathers, Jofeh chastised him for his lack of professional attire and wanted him to change in an anteroom.

In time, Jofeh came to be disliked by everyone. He was more arrogant than aristocratic, smoking a pipe all the time and keeping his distance not only from the shop floor but also from almost everyone in management whom he hadn't personally hired. "People didn't like him because he didn't want to become too 'matey,'" said Mike Jackson. "He looked down at motorcyclists."

One of Jofeh's first steps seemed positive on the surface. At the suggestion of private consultants McKinsey, Jofeh decided to open a separate R&D studio, a step Hopwood had long recommended. The two men — not friends but thrown into battle together — ventured out one day in spring 1967 to inspect Umberslade Hall, an old manor home in nearby Hockley Heath made of handsome brick and limestone trim and leaded glass windows everywhere. Peacocks often roamed the grounds, and there was even a sculpture garden and pond in front featuring a nude limestone statue. Jofeh thought it at once regal and pastoral, a perfect retreat. It would be an R&D facility to rival what Honda was doing but in the English way. Jofeh populated the Group Engineering Centre, as it was officially dubbed, largely with those engineers whom he knew from the aircraft industry and young university graduates. It's said that very few of the new hires rode motorcycles. Mike Jackson says the opening of Umberslade Hall held promise. "In one way, that was a very good idea to have your R&D separate from the factory so your thinking could be very clear. And being out in the country they could do testing."

But Hopwood found many of the rooms dark — very poor for the kind of drafting tables still in use in the years before computer-assisted design. There was at least one banquet-sized area where many prototypical bikes sat on pneumatic stands, not so different from what a sculptor's studio might look like if shared by many sculptors. The whole effect was oddly divorced from the hum and din of a real factory, which Hopwood decided was a good reminder after all of where any babies would really be born, no matter where conception took place.

In time, at least 150 workers would staff Umberslade Hall. Cost to the factory was between 500,000 and 1.5 million pounds annually, based on varying estimates. But Hopwood and his chief engineering assistant, Hele, never moved there.

The Triumph division also began a skunk works investigation into a new, Wankel rotary-engined machine, which the BSA Group had licensed from a German company. Why play catch-up with the Japanese when you could leap-frog them with new technology? It must have seemed like a brilliant idea — an ultra-modern rotary engine that would do away with pistons, valves, and other reciprocating parts in a four-stroke motor that were the source of all the terrible vibration that had long afflicted British bikes. But engineers struggled to get the required power and never overcame serious heating problems. One problem? The fresh air charge in the carburetor was used to cool the cylinders, which upset any hope of a constant fuel-air ratio needed for clean combustion and smooth running. The prototype also broke down a lot. Pieces brought to Hopwood for inspection after this or that latest disaster were wryly dubbed "the burnt offerings." Nevertheless, the project continued on the back burner.

In addition to the efforts at Umberslade Hall and the Wankel project, the semi-retired Edward Turner, who maintained a non-executive seat on the BSA board, was given space in an old factory in Redditch to work on a new 350 cc overhead cam twin that might compete directly with the Japanese in the burgeoning middleweight sport bike market. If Honda was mounting a frontal assault on the British, maybe it could be given reason to pause in the face of a strong counterpunch.

It was a strategy, a battle plan even. The British would fight back. But Umberslade Hall was no Whitehall. In time, Umberslade was to earn the mocking pseudonym "Slumberglade Hall" because of its slow progress. Opened in 1968, Umberslade Hall announced its first fruit only in November 1970 at a press launch at London's Royal Lancaster Hotel, a recently completed steel and glass mid-rise building overlooking Hyde Park near the heart of the city. The soiree attracted more than 350 guests, including industry personnel and reporters and photographers from the mainstream media. There was entertainment (music by pop group The Young Generation, assorted dancers, and a comedian) plus a fully catered meal. The party cost a tidy 15,000 pounds.[9]

All in all, there would be 13 new and/or improved models from the BSA Group, the largest roll-out in motorcycle history, or so the company claimed. In fact, the models were hardly "all new," though there were some new features. The Victor motor, no longer a match for the European two-strokes on the Grand Prix circuit, had nevertheless been enlarged to 500 cc and was, in fact, the best four-stroke off-road production motorcycle in the world, better than anything the Japanese offered at the time. This latest Victor, by then officially known as the B50 model, was also marketed as the Gold Star even though it had no connection to the original, was strong, light, and fast, if oddly styled, with a foolishly small alloy gas tank and a large, black muffler with a garish, perforated chrome heat guard. The 500 cc off-road and "dual purpose" market wasn't large, however, and the bike's strengths could only really be appreciated by expert riders, so it was all a bit beside the point.

There was a new chassis announced for the flagship twins incorporating an "oil in frame" feature drawn from works racing practice; the innovative Rickman brothers had also been using a similar system for years. Instead of needing a separate oil tank, the oil filler would lead directly to a four-inch-diameter tubular backbone. The large backbone was an innovation that provided great strength and rigidity with simplicity of design and is often credited to independent chassis designer Rob North, who had been building custom road-racing frames for the triples on a freelance basis. The "oil in frame" feature, usually credited to Dr. Stefan Bauer (the same Bauer who had helped to create the Isolastic frame for Norton), was almost superfluous, however. Doing away with a separate oil tank would save a bit of weight and even simplify production somewhat, but it was mind-numbing esoterica for the evolving motorcycle enthusiast, who just wanted to get on the saddle, push a starter button, and go. Worse, the new frames were too tall for many riders, with a seat height of 34.5 inches, at least two to three inches higher than any other large-capacity road machine. The new frame handled quite well, but what good was race-bred handling if riders couldn't touch the pavement with their toes at stoplights? The brake and suspension components were upgraded nicely — still no disc brakes, though — and there was no electric starting either. All in all, the new models represented an extremely poor return on investment in Umberslade Hall, and still there was no truly new engine.

The crowd at the Royal Lancaster that evening was not impressed. Jack Sangster, motorcycle industry godfather and retired chairman of the board at BSA Group, said flatly that the range would not be successful — and this was before it was understood that several of the models would not in fact ever be produced. "There wasn't a word of applause when [the motorcycles] were introduced," recalled Wilf Harrison.

Don Brown, the long-time Johnson Motors and later BSA sales executive, watched events unfold with dismay. "I was getting upset at the introduction," he said. "The more I was there, the more I was getting upset." The heady years of the British motorcycle industry now seemed a distant memory. Besides the invasion from the East, there was the enemy within. The first warning signs of an imminent collapse came in 1968, when a combination of labour troubles and missed production deadlines by a host of subcontractors caused BSA and Triumph to ship motorcycles to America late in the spring, which meant the firm missed much of the "selling season," as the British always called it. This is likely why the new triples weren't seen in American showrooms until June that year. The company was forced to buy back several thousand machines, mostly twins, and dump them on European markets at a loss. Typically, the British firms would produce new model year bikes in the late fall and winter for early spring delivery in the United States, when the short selling season would begin. Money would be going out, but not coming in, just like farmers worldwide had to operate. Missing much of the market in 1968 led to an indebtedness that BSA was to carry with it until the end. Joe Heaton noted that the crisis ate into the company's reserves, which stood at a high-water mark of 16.9 million pounds sterling as of August 30, 1968. The reserves stood at 12.9 million pounds sterling as of 30 August, 1970, but fell precipitously to 4.7 million pounds sterling 12 months later, which covered the period when the company failed to deliver most of the Royal Lancaster Hotel models to dealers. They were "nil" by August 30, 1973. Yet Heaton is also clever in asking why were reserves so high in the mid-1960s to begin with? He argues that much of the reserves should have been invested in new products earlier and/or that BSA Group should have lowered profit margins to increase market share against the rising Japanese threat.[10]

The company also made an expensive decision to continue fielding a Grand Prix motocross team throughout the decade — the last British company to do so in the senior 500 cc class. New BSA top rider John Banks did well, missing the 1968 championship by just one point, but the Europeans had finally mastered two-stroke engine design and were to win every large-capacity world championship from 1966 until the Japanese attacked this sport, too, in the 1970s. The Europeans had already been winning in the 250 cc class with fast two-strokes for years.

BSA had, in fact, anticipated the threat from the two-strokes, countering with an all-new titanium-framed Victor model in 1966. Harry Sturgeon was its biggest backer, according to Jeff Smith, who was forced to actually ride the bike. "Sturgeon said [in September 1965], 'Here's what we're going to do. We're going to put together a team of engineers that's going to give you the best and lightest machine available that's going to be the basis of our range of machines for the next 5 to 10 years,'" Smith recalled. Smith, Ernie Webster, Brian Martin, and seven other engineers formed a committee to help develop and evaluate progress of the machine, and they were given a budget of 30,000 pounds for the initial prototype.

Many of BSA's engineers had previously worked in Britain's substantial aviation industry and had experience with the ultra-lightweight metal. In time, they built a machine that weighed about 202 pounds — an astoundingly low figure for a four-stroke, heavyweight-class motocross machine. The bike proved somewhat competitive but was not a world beater. A frame designed with steel tubing in mind wouldn't necessarily work if built from a different material. This was one lesson learned. In particular, the titanium off-road frame was "whippy," meaning that it would flex under heavy loading, then snap back, making it hard to control. Plus, the frames could only be welded up in expensive vacuum chambers. There was no chance this frame could be commercially viable, and the project was largely abandoned after the 1968 race season, another costly failure for the company.

BSA and Triumph recovered, if only briefly, from the 1968 export mini-crisis. Besides the launch of the Honda four-cylinder street bike in 1969, the 1970s got off to a disastrous start, largely because of investment in the Ariel 3, a three-wheeled moped introduced in June 1970. The Ariel 3, made by BSA, looked a lot like mobility scooters for overweight or disabled people in use today. It was targeted to shoppers who were told they could carry up to 50 pounds of groceries in the back. The problems with the Ariel 3 were myriad. The small, two-stroke motors were made in Holland, and all 20,000 samples in an early shipment were prone to overheating. Worse, the trikes were unstable. The rear axle was hinged in such a way as to allow the wheels to pivot left or right after the rider initiated a turn with the handlebars, but this led to decreasing-radius turns many riders found difficult to manage. The trikes often had a slight weave when going down the road above 25 mph too. In the event, very few were sold upon introduction, and the Ariel 3 was quickly withdrawn. BSA had planned production of 2,000 of the three-wheeled mopeds weekly but instead lost 2 million pounds on the venture.[11]

The BSA Beeza and Triumph Tigress, the Tina, the BSA Beagle, the Ariel Pixie, and now the Ariel 3 — in 15 years, the company had repeatedly tried to enter the scooter market and had failed miserably each time. Think of Ford Motor Company introducing not one Edsel but five such failures in a single generation.

But the worst thing was Edward Turner's double overhead cam, 350 cc motorcycle, the identical BSA Fury and Triumph Bandit. The original frame, as designed by Turner, was too light and fragile and was replaced by a more advanced, heavily triangulated chassis designed by famed frame maker Ken Sprayson. Whereas the big English companies had spurned independent frame makers Don and Derek Rickman, now they couldn't avoid such freelancers. Triangulation of frame members provides great strength with a minimum of steel tubing and welding and was state-of-the-art practice in the 1960s and '70s.

Prototype Fury engines produced up to 34 horsepower at 9,000 rpm, and the engines had a racy, forward look to them. Production models were to have contemporary five-speed transmissions and optional electric starting too. Yet Turner's engine also had to be modified in the interest of increased reliability. "On the test bench, the prototype smashed its way through two crankshafts and gulped down four pints of oil during the equivalent of 100 miles," wrote one observer. "It was noisy, it rattled and was self-destructive — within 4,000 miles the whole power unit had to be rebuilt four times."[12]

Doug Hele was called in to fix the motor. He quickly dumped the gear drive for the overhead cams in favour of a simpler chain drive and beefed up the fragile crankshaft. Hopwood, the senior engineer still on the full-time payroll at the BSA Group, refused to have anything to do with the machine, perhaps hoping it would fail.

It was clear that Jofeh wanted a final prototype ready for the Lancaster Hotel press launch, and the bike in production by the following spring, come hell or high water. Amazingly, he ordered expensive tooling for this "world beater" before any long-term testing had been completed. An exciting ad campaign was launched in America for the Fury too. Both a street scrambler with upswept exhaust pipes and a road model were presented, and the pre-production samples were pretty — lean, smartly painted in white and plum, and modern overall. A complete parts replacement book was also published ahead of actual production. But the bikes never were produced. After a total investment of some 1 million pounds in this project alone, BSA killed production rather than commit further to it. The reason? Hopwood said it needed a new engine built from scratch. The more likely reason? BSA accountants surmised that the actual selling price in America would be nearly double that for the similar Honda 350 cc overhead cam twin in any case. It was Edward Turner's last great, unambiguous, indefensible, completely dismal failure.[13]

Although up-to-date profit-and-loss statements weren't available to the Lancaster Hotel guests that night in November 1970, many insiders suspected what the accountants would disclose in time — BSA and Triumph were deeply in debt and were to lose 13 million pounds more between 1971 and mid-1973, when the BSA Group was dissolved.[14]

Jofeh was challenged several times in the months both before and after the press launch about rumours that the new models would not, in fact, be ready in time. Just one of the myriad problems was a strike prompted by a missed payroll, and other delays were caused by suppliers who failed to meet their deadlines, perhaps because they were nervous about being paid. This was not merely an echo of the 1968 crisis but the other shoe dropping. Then there was a crisis caused by a new computer that kept ordering some parts "just in time" style, except that the parts weren't needed because production wasn't yet up and running in the winter of 1970–71. In spite of all this mounting evidence, Jofeh continued to assert that production would begin soon and that all bikes would sell well. By March 1971, American dealers began demanding to know why the promised new models hadn't arrived. Most would never arrive, in fact. It all led to a ripple effect — the dealers had borrowed against the spring selling season, and they wouldn't be able to repay their debts. Back in England, Barclays Bank, which had financed much of BSA's development costs and tool purchases, was getting even more nervous. Private consultants brought in by Chairman and CEO

Eric Turner discovered that the company owed more (over 20 million pounds) than it could reasonably project in gross revenues. Under British law and the company's own articles of association, that meant BSA was trading illegally.[15]

Reports differ, but Jofeh either resigned or was sacked on July 8, 1971. Eric Turner himself was forced to resign later that year. The company was in free fall. Barclays agreed to a rescue of 10 million pounds on the condition that Lord Hartley Shawcross, the respected former Labour MP from St. Helens and England's chief prosecutor at the Nazi war crimes trial in Nuremberg, be elevated to "non-executive" chairman of the board, meaning that he would not run the company on a day-to-day basis but have to sign off on all important decisions. Shawcross was at once controversial and much respected, a larger-than-life figure who wasn't afraid to tell people of any political persuasion to bugger off. He was born in Geissen, Germany, in 1902; his English-born father was a professor of English at a local college at the time. The family came from money, but their politics had often been left leaning. Nonetheless, Shawcross was granted a life peerage in 1959 and spent much of the remainder of his life serving on the boards of various prominent companies, such as Shell, EMI (the music recording company), and Times Newspapers. The fact that Shawcross was appointed to such a high-profile position in the motorcycle industry illustrated just how important that industry was to both the national economy and the national psyche. Brian Eustace would become the chief executive officer of the company in terms of day-to-day operations. Hopwood replaced Jofeh in the motorcycle division. The workforce at Small Heath was trimmed from 4,500 to 1,500 in 1971, and several subsidiaries were sold off to raise cash. In late 1972, part of the factory on Armoury Road, plus the locally famous BSA sports fields, were sold to the Birmingham Corporation for 1 million pounds.[16] BSA marque production at Small Heath dropped from 6,286 bikes in the third quarter of 1971 (August–October) to 202 bikes built in the first quarter of 1972 (February–April), when the fabrication of complete motorcycles at Small Heath all but ended.[16]

Emergency makeovers were performed on the model line, most notably at Triumph, which had the better name in America. All big twins kept the oil-in-frame chassis for 1972, but seat height was lowered, and plans were made to bump the Triumph Bonneville to 750 cc capacity, though that wasn't to happen until the 1973 model year. The green light was also given to a rogue USA design, the Craig Vetter "X-75 Hurricane," as it came to be known. Vetter, "a long-legged hippie-type with hair to match, dressed in the requisite blue jeans and T-shirt," according to Don Brown, was a young University of Illinois design student who made motorcycle fairings by hand in nearby Rantoul, Illinois. He was contacted by Brown shortly after the Rocket 3 and Trident were introduced and offered the chance to come up with custom body work for the very fast but very staid-looking bikes. Vetter would be paid $27 per hour — but only if his bike were put into production. He bought a one-way airplane ticket to Nutley, New Jersey, to pick up a Rocket 3, which he then rode back to Illinois.

In time, Vetter created a swoopy, one-piece tank and rear fender section of orange-pigmented plastic for the bike and three full exhausts stacked on the right side of the chassis at a jaunty angle. "I am the first of the 'Plastic Generation' of designers," Vetter later boasted. "We plastic designers are able to see more free flowing shapes, and are not as restricted in our thinking as, say, metal-stamp designers."[18]

The bike proved to be a "love it or hate it" affair, being somewhat derivative of the raked-out chopper look with a small peanut gas tank featured in the 1969 film *Easy Rider*. When a prototype was completed in 1969 or 1970, the X-75 was covered in bubble wrap and shipped to England for evaluation, but it languished in a warehouse for several months. Hopwood dismissed the styling as "trendy," and Eric Turner was so angry with Brown for authorizing the project he demanded to see a written contract. The bike was put into production during the tumultuous 1973 season only, and Vetter was paid $12,000 for his design work. Not many were sold, but the bike is highly collectible today.

These were stopgaps, of course, simply updating existing models. Hopwood and Hele also pushed ahead with design drawings for an all-new modular line of engines built around multiples of the same 200 cc cylinder, but nothing ever came of it. Events in Coventry and London were to overtake everybody.

It was the autumn of 1972. Mr. Poore, Chairman of Norton Villiers, was called to the Industrial Development Unit of the Department of Trade and Industry, recently formed to administer the new Industry Act, and informed that the Department had been advised by Lord Shawcross, Chairman of BSA, that BSA would shortly be unable to meet its obligations and, unless assistance was forthcoming from the Department, Barclays Bank would be asked to appoint a receiver. Mr. Poore was asked whether Norton Villiers would consider a merger in order to save the important motorcycle export potential of BSA/Triumph, then running at some $40 million annually, which it appeared otherwise would be lost. Officials of the Department explained that investment of public funds for this purpose could be made under the Industry Act but section 8 would have to be used for the first time. All previous support under the Act had been given under section 7, where the primary objective was the maintenance of employment in a development area. Section 8 was for a different purpose entirely, namely the promotion of industry in any area in the national interest when for some reason adequate private sector funds could not be obtained.[19]

Thus begins one of the most extraordinary documents in British industrial history. Dennis Poore, dashing young race car driver, distinguished Royal Air Force commander, the saviour of Norton motorcycles, a man who was somebody in the city with offices at 1 Love Lane, London, had been reduced to making his case in public, bypassing the media of the day, publishing his own booklet in order to explain why he was a terribly aggrieved man and why the government must stop a group of 200 or so radicals who had illegally occupied the Triumph motorcycle factory in Meriden, blocking the delivery of thousands of completed motorcycles intended for export.

The booklet was paid for by NVT and, according to Keith Blair, had been dictated in one evening by Poore himself. When this document was released in the summer of 1974, the workers' sit-in had been regular news in the *Times* of London and other British newspapers for months and had been a regular feature on the nightly television news across the country. Begun in September 1973, the sit-in was to last 18 months, making it one of the longest such industrial actions in British history.

The Department of Trade and Industry had indeed met with Norton Villiers and BSA leaders in the latter company's impressive boardroom in Birmingham on November 30, 1972. The talks were considered so secret that notes from the meeting referred to Norton Villiers as "Zebra" and BSA as "Longlegs," according to Hopwood. Various plans were discussed, but they all called for BSA to acquire Norton Villiers and for Manganese Bronze Holdings to acquire all of BSA's non-motorcycle subsidiaries, which were still substantial. Poore would continue as head of MBH *and* become head of the new, as yet unnamed, motorcycle company. Details of such a plan were circulated among the principals on March 14, 1973, yet the equation changed radically when BSA share prices plummeted from 18 pence to 5 pence on that day, losing 2 million pounds in stock value, and trading was suspended. An inquiry held later found the nominal cause of the drop to be a "bear" raid in which a group of private investors offered to sell a large number of BSA shares they didn't possess, hoping to depress the stock price so that they could scoop up shares at a reduced price and deliver them to their own buyers at the agreed-upon price on "settlement day." An official government inquiry concluded that the stock manipulators didn't include anyone connected to the eventual merger (i.e., it wasn't Poore).[20]

Joe Heaton believes the spur for the stock market crisis was Edward Turner, who published a damning letter in the *Daily Telegraph* (London) on March 7, 1973, in which he accused Lord Shawcross of mismanagement. "Lord Shawcross is a distinguished lawyer, but this does not mean he is an expert on motorcycles," wrote Turner. "Machines sell on the whim of fashionable young men. These fads are constantly changing. BSA Triumph are still trying to flog off the stuff I designed 30 years and more ago."[21]

Whatever the cause of the stock crash, the terms of the merger eventually were changed, much to Poore's advantage. BSA was not worthless, but it was worth less. On June 8th, the *Times* of London reported that the Department of Trade and Industry would invest 4.87 million pounds sterling in the new motorcycle venture, to be called Norton Villiers Triumph (NVT). The government, along with Poore's Manganese Bronze Holdings and shareholders in the BSA Group, would own the new entity. This was indeed a merger — neither Norton nor BSA put any money into the new motorcycle company, and both benefited from the government investment. BSA Group would also sell its substantial non-motorcycle holdings to Poore for 3.5 million pounds — that's the only money BSA shareholders would get. The new motorcycle company would be incorporated separately from MBH, meaning that even if it failed MBH would be responsible for none of it, and MBH would keep the non-motorcycle divisions of BSA no matter what. They included the BSA Metal Components Division, Carbodies Limited (which made the iconic London taxis), BSA Guns (the piled arms, of course), and some other interests.[22]

Shawcross and Eustace resigned, and Poore quickly settled on a policy called the "two-factory model," meaning either Small Heath or Meriden would have to go, and the survivor would join forces with his plant in Wolverhampton, where the Norton Commando was largely produced. Such emergency surgery had been broached before — BSA management itself had been advised as far back as 1971 to close one or the other of its factories and consolidate production in the surviving plant. One team of consultants pointedly suggested shuttering the main plant at Small Heath, in part out of fear of provoking the well-known militancy of the Meriden workers but also because they discovered that BSA could buy lots of components from outside suppliers more cheaply than making them itself. BSA was more of a true manufacturing plant; Triumph was more of a final assembly plant and might accommodate the new plan better.

Poore wanted to close Meriden, however. The Meriden plant made the popular Bonneville model and the chassis for the Rocket 3 and Trident models, but the actual motors for the latter were produced in Small Heath. Plus, the BSA factory was more modern on the inside, with more overhead conveyors and timed delivery of parts. Poore always denied that he wanted to shut down Meriden because of the unions or the high wages the workers had won for themselves over the years, which were significantly higher than at Small Heath or Wolverhampton, but he may have been disingenuous in saying so.

Still, Poore tried a partial solution first. In July 1973, exactly 232 Triumph employees accepted "voluntary redundancy," which is the equivalent to a buy-out scheme in American business, costing NVT about 100,000 pounds. The deal was personally negotiated by Poore and the Meriden shop stewards in an effort to save the remaining jobs there.[23]

Two months later, on September 14th, Poore met with a further group of workers in the Meriden factory canteen, announcing from a tabletop that he would have to close the factory after all. He tried to explain to the stunned, murmuring workers that there would be a "run-down" at the factory lasting until February 1974, but after that the factory would be closed. All in all, about 1,750 remaining employees would lose their positions. Sales projections for the three remaining models in NVT's catalogue — the Commando, Trident, and Bonneville — didn't warrant all the production capacity available, he said. The BSA twins and single-cylinder model, as well as the Triumph 500 cc twin, were all consigned to the scrap heap. The Rocket 3 version of the triple would also not be continued — indeed, the BSA brand was being killed off. So much for "one in four is a BSA," the battle cry of the 1930s.

"Mr. Poore read the closure announcement to the assembled meeting of some 80 stewards in the canteen," according to an NVT summary of the meeting. "Mr. [Leslie] Huckfield [Labour MP for Nuneaton] and the district officials of several unions were also present. Simultaneous announcements were made at Small

Heath and Wolverhampton. After a short recess, asked for by the district union officials, the management party returned to the canteen to find that Mr. Huckfield had taken charge of the meeting and was holding the microphone on the rostrum. . . ."[24]

Huckfield, as well as Christopher Chataway, the minister for industrial development who had negotiated the original BSA-Norton merger, publicly denounced the planned closure. Several days later the factory was occupied by 200 Triumph employees, including almost all the shop stewards. The gates were locked, 2,650 completed machines were taken hostage, and management was barred from entering the premises. Within a month, the union stewards announced they had a plan — they would buy the Meriden factory from NVT, form a workers' co-operative, and continue to make the Bonneville on their own.

John R. Nelson, a former service manager at Triumph and a managing director of the future Meriden co-op for some 18 months, later said, "The sit-in was a spontaneous reaction to what was considered to be previous years of deliberate and planned political and financial neglect by the parent company ultimately causing its own collapse, and the subsequent instant announcement by Dennis Poore of the immediate closure of the factory. The sit-in was to preserve the name of Triumph, and the Bonneville in particular."[25] Poore wanted to get a court injunction and call in the police to evict the protesters — it simply was an illegal occupation — but leaders inside the Conservative government then in power implored him to continue to negotiate. Overall labour relations were very poor in England at the time. First, there was a looming miners' strike, and the government didn't want to fan the flames. Then there was the Arab oil boycott in late 1973, followed by the so-called "Winter of Our Discontent" as not only miners but also railway workers and power station employees went on strike. The entire country was soon put on the "three-day week" to conserve energy, and new elections had to be called in March 1974.

An ex-film student who visited the factory during the troubles told his story to a socialist publication. "I filmed the Triumph sit-in in Meriden when I was at film school," recalled Mike Rosen.

"There was one guy who was a Labour Party shop steward who locked the gates. There were all these crates full of bikes in the factory that was being occupied. I asked the bloke what he was going to do about that and he said, 'Well, we control it so it's up to us.' The workers had a sense that they made stuff that was valuable and you could see a change among them. You can only hope that the anti-globalisation movement today will go in that direction."[26]

Negotiations dragged on for more than a year, and several plans were concocted. For a short period, a few completed Bonnevilles were doled out on a daily basis as an inducement to continue talks, yet NVT was forced to spend half a million pounds to make new jigs and other parts for the Trident chassis and install them at Small Heath. Once Trident deliveries could be resumed, mostly to the United States, sales proved difficult. Not only was the Honda 750 still strong, but Kawasaki had also introduced a true world beater in the 900 cc, four-cylinder Z1 in 1972. The latter bike was faster by far than anything else on the market and looked good, too, with an elongated, zoomy gas tank and tapered sport fenders offered in chrome.

Mike Jackson was ordered to sell off 1,000 Tridents in the United States for whatever price he could get. "I remember that if a dealer committed to 25 there was a considerable further reduction in price," he said. "We were in a desperate state."

Things seemed at a stalemate when a change of government on March 6, 1974, occurred. Harold Wilson was elected to head a new Labour government, and Anthony Wedgwood "Tony" Benn was made minister of trade and industry. Benn was the most left-leaning man in government at the time. The balance of power had shifted.

Benn was committed to "industrial democracy," part of the Labour Party election manifesto, or platform, as it would be called in the United States. He also spoke of "participation" and "control" by workers in their industrial destiny and said it was all "inevitable," sounding very much like people who said socialism was the wave of the future. Benn saw a workers' co-op at Meriden as a good place to start. "I hoped people from the shop stewards' movement would begin to formulate their demands," Benn wrote in a diary early in the sit-in. "The real test [will be] the Meriden affair."[27]

Years later a senior union leader at Triumph claimed they hadn't really meant to establish a co-op at Meriden. It was just a ploy to get Poore to keep the factory open. "There was never any intention to start the Co-op," said Bill Lapworth, senior official of the Transport and General Workers Union (TGWU), which represented almost all the Meriden workers, "but we were convinced on business terms that Meriden was best placed to stay open as opposed to BSA at Small Heath."[28]

Benn was a complex man and was to become the most famous socialist in Britain in modern times. He gave up his family peerage, which would have entitled him to a seat in the House of Lords, to run for Parliament. Always quotable, he once listed his education as "still in progress" in a government biography. He was, of course, educated at the best schools from his youth, including at Oxford for university.

Benn soon found an ally in Geoffrey Robinson, the managing director of Jaguar in Coventry from 1973 to 1975. Robinson has been described as a "Fabian socialist," meaning he was one of the upper classes that supported a gradual and evolutionary approach to ending capitalism, and later was to be a primary backer of Tony Blair and New Labour. Robinson was elected to Parliament for Coventry North West, a so-called "safe" Labour seat in 1976, and served three decades.

"The co-operative's value as a social and industrial relations experiment is by far the most important aspect of what we are trying to do," Robinson wrote to Benn in June 1974. "Its relevance is to point a new way forward in terms of whether with a wider system of ownership, labour relations can be got right, whether restrictive and other malpractices can be eliminated, and whether higher levels of production and productivity can be obtained and sustained."[29]

Poore was aghast. When he was asked to merge with the BSA Group's motorcycle division, he expected to sell the company's most legendary machine, the Bonneville, as well as the Trident and Commando. Plus, he owned the Triumph brand now — how could he cede that to the Meriden workers or, rather more oddly, share it like some concubine?

Just as the government had financed the NVT takeover, so too Benn proposed that the government would have to fund the workers' purchase of the Meriden factory and rights to manufacture the Bonneville. *Private Eye*, the satirical British magazine, famously called this "Benn and the Art of Motorcycle Maintenance," after a popular book title of the day. It was only 30 years later, after official cabinet meeting notes from the Wilson administration were unsealed, that Benn's true intentions were revealed — he wanted to nationalize most of Britain's industry or at least allow workers to take direct control of as much of it as possible. Meriden was the lever he'd push first, and he could mask his socialist bent by claiming he was doing this for Britain. Wilson, though nominally a socialist, didn't think government could produce better results than the free market, and he wanted to evict the man who had proven to be a rebellious protégé. Benn had other supporters on the left, however, and his scheme moved forward.[30]

The press largely turned against Poore; increasingly, he was described as a "predator" and an "asset stripper" who wanted to make Triumphs in Small Heath and sacrifice the jobs of about 1,750 men and women in Meriden, all the while keeping the BSA subsidiaries for himself. The terms of the Industry Act were all but forgotten in the din — Poore's charge was not to save jobs but to save an industry, exactly as he claimed. At a press launch in late 1973 for the limited 1974 range of models he still hoped to produce, Poore was cornered by a journalist who accused him of being an asset stripper to his face. Poore famously retorted, "What assets do you actually mean?"[31]

Geoffrey Robinson led the workers' negotiating team, with Benn's blessing, even though he still ran Jaguar in nearby Coventry. Certainly, Robinson was a match for fellow industrialist Poore both intellectually and in political circles. A tentative agreement was worked out. The thorny "Triumph" brand issue would be resolved this way: the Meriden workers would produce Bonnevilles and sell them to Poore, who would resell the bikes under the Triumph name, which he would continue to own. For its part, the government would give Poore another 1.1 million pounds and essentially forgive 365,000 pounds in "dividends" NVT otherwise might owe the government as a major stockholder in that concern. The co-operative would get 4.95 million pounds, close to the maximum allowed under the Industry Act and the same amount invested earlier in NVT itself.

On July 30, 1974, the *Times* announced that Poore had accepted this offer. Yet it was not so — more snags were revealed, and several revisions of the plan were advanced and then shot down. Still, a divide had been bridged — supporting the co-operative was now official government policy, and Poore had agreed in principle to the concept of sharing Triumph.

On November 8, 1974, Benn visited the BSA workers at Small Heath, who were increasingly nervous that *their* factory would be shuttered if the Meriden factory stayed open. The leading voice for the workingman in Britain was not well received. "Mr. Anthony Wedgwood Benn, Secretary of State for Industry, who made a hurried trip to Birmingham yesterday in an attempt to persuade the 1,200 workers that the [co-op] scheme did not threaten their jobs, was given a rough reception," reported the *Times* correspondent. "Mr. Benn was consistently heckled and pressed by workers to give assurances about future job security."[32]

Benn also visited workers at the Commando facility in Wolverhampton, where he received much the same treatment. All he could do was say that, yes, he wanted to save all motorcycle industry jobs, not just the ones in Meriden. Yet few knowledgeable people believed the industry could support three factories — there was just too much capacity.

For their part, the Meriden workers accused Poore of "engineering" the worker opposition at Small Heath and Wolverhampton, and on one occasion several surrounded and menaced Hugh Palin, the NVT company spokesman who made an appearance at the Triumph factory.[33]

On February 1, 1975, another tentative deal was announced in which NVT would sell the Triumph factory and manufacturing rights to a workers' co-operative. NVT would receive 4.2 million pounds, and the government would guarantee 8 million pounds in export credits to sell the Bonneville along with the Commando and Trident overseas. Still, the sit-in wasn't to end until March, and NVT was in deep trouble itself by then, recording a loss of 7.4 million pounds sterling in the 20 months between the official start of the merger and the end of the sit-in. Poore demanded that the government give him even more aid. "When the Government unilaterally changed the agreed plan by requiring the continuation of Meriden by [the] cooperative, the undertakings given to the NVT workforce that their jobs would not be endangered were given in the full knowledge, supported by detailed figures by the NVT management at the time, that these undertakings could only be honoured by a substantial further investment in NVT," Poore wrote in the *Times*.[34]

What to do? It was in 1975 that Parliament commissioned the Boston Consulting Group to study the future of the British motorcycle industry. The report noted the failure of the industry's "segment retreat" strategy in which it abandoned one market segment after another in which it couldn't compete, and it emphasized the advantage Honda enjoyed in selling first to a huge home market, which taught it lessons in cost-efficient manufacturing techniques. The consultants noted that, in spite of some profitable years in the 1960s, the industry had actually been in decline for about 15 years, both in terms of market share and in terms of absolute units produced. Most damningly, they noted the overall reputation for poor reliability throughout much of the British range. The best model for success the consultants could think of was BMW in West Germany — make a high-quality product in moderate numbers and sell it for a premium price. The current British lineup wouldn't justify the kind of premium BMWs commanded, however, so new models would have to be developed, the report concluded. Or perhaps a modular system was the way to go — the consultants knew of Hopwood's modular scheme, which was quickly abandoned when NVT was formed in 1973. Any plan would take about five years and require millions in additional investments. Would success be guaranteed? No — the consultants were just suggesting alternative strategies.

It didn't matter. The government didn't listen to any of it except, perhaps, the parts that talked about millions more in investment and years of patience. Instead, the government decided to fund the co-operative and refused further aid to NVT to help produce machines or export guarantees to help sell them abroad. Poore's reaction? It was like an implosion. First, Poore announced that he'd close the Wolverhampton factory and produce the Commando at Small Heath, along with the Trident, which he would still own. That announcement, however, led to a four-month workers' sit-in at Wolverhampton that Poore facetiously lauded in print, suggesting that Tony Benn might have to save those jobs too. He no longer cared, actually. In November, Dennis Poore, the erstwhile saviour of the British motorcycle industry, began the process of dissolving NVT, the last conglomerate, earning for himself another derisive title, that of the man who "killed" the industry.

Norman Vanhouse, the long-time BSA off-road rider who had won a gold medal in the 1952 International Six Days Trial on a stock Star Twin model, recalled going to the public auction at Small Heath several years after the closure. The last complete bikes to roll off the assembly line there were a batch of Triumph Tridents in white livery headed for Saudi Arabia; that was on a warm Wednesday evening in July 1975. This grey day in 1977 or '78 the remaining equipment went for scrap, Vanhouse said, and as he walked through these new catacombs and dragged his feet on the wood plank floors he looked for something actually useful to buy for himself. In one of the offices he saw it — a manual typewriter that he bought for five pounds, which he used to write a history of the BSA competition shop several years later.

Enough Commando parts remained at Wolverhampton or in the pipeline from various suppliers to complete 1,500 additional bikes. Poore cleverly offered the official receiver a lump sum for the lot, which was accepted, and sales of the Commando continued through 1979 in one guise or another. Frank Melling, the young hippy journalist who had stood up to Lionel Jofeh in the BSA boardroom in 1971 and continued his love of motorcycles all his adult life, recalled in 2007 what happened to the last

Commando ever built. "The last Commando was sold to a customer who insisted on having legendary Norton tuner Ray Petty hand it over to him at a formal ceremony. [It] was the last Commando ever to leave the factory, except that works manager John Pedley allegedly took exception to a 'civilian' having the final Commando and had his workers build another one, with an even higher engine number and frame number, for his own personal use. This tale was related by an extremely well-connected ex-Norton man and might well be true."[35]

Epilogue

It was a black day in 1971 when Bert Hopwood called his most famous employee up to his second-floor office on Armoury Road to give him the bad news. "He told me I better quit now, because if I waited six months there won't be any money left in the till to pay my pension," recalled Jeff Smith, the long-time BSA rider and two-time world motocross champion. To make things more palatable, Hopwood said Smith could keep three of his racing bikes and enough spares to carry him through to the end of the season. Wisely, Smith accepted the offer.

While Hopwood continued to labour on in the struggling British motorcycle industry for several more years, Smith soon moved to North America, where he helped Canadian snowmobile company Bombardier develop a new line of off-road motorcycles. The company put him up in the Showboat Casino in Las Vegas for six weeks in January 1972 so he could test several prototypes in the nearby desert. Smith took his assignment seriously and recommended several changes, and the orange-and-black "Can-Am" motorcycles, as the brand was called, were introduced in 1973.

After leaving Can-Am, Smith was appointed executive director of the struggling American Historic Racing Motorcycle Association, which stages road-racing and dirt-racing competitions on vintage motorcycles across the country. Smith and his wife, Irene, the sister of early BSA motocross star John Draper, partly ran the organization out of their Wisconsin home and saw membership ranks swell by the thousands.

Smith continues to travel widely and ride competitively.

Edward Turner died a sour, lonely old man in 1973. In what may have been the last interview he ever gave from his apartment near London's Gatwick Airport that year, he said, "I'd like to produce a real good 'four' today, a modern 'four.' I had a good look at the Honda four. There's nothing to beat. It's a bloody awful motorcycle when all is said and done."

Many top road racers of the era such as John Surtees and Jim Redman have found a second life by making appearances on the classic and vintage motorcycle circuit. Geoff Duke started a motorsports video company with his son and lives on the Isle of Man. Mike Hailwood made one of the most famous "comebacks" in all of sports history by winning his class on a 900 cc Ducati motorcycle at the Isle of Man in 1978. He was killed on March 23, 1981, along with his nine-year-old daughter, Michelle, while driving the family to buy pizza near his home in England.

Frank Melling has continued to write about motorcycles for a variety of publications all his adult life, and he runs the popular Thundersprint, an annual classic bike revival in Cheshire. Brian Slark is the archivist at the Barber Vintage Motorsports Museum in Birmingham, Alabama. Michael "Old Mike" Jackson continued in the motorcycle trade and today is a consultant for Bonhams, the arts and antiques auctioneers. Don Brown has a garage full of motorcycle memorabilia he promises to sort out one day.

Norton Villiers Triumph was officially dissolved in 1978, but Poore still had deep pockets. He — or rather his company, NVT — had received 2.3 million pounds from the government for letting go of Meriden and the Bonneville model, which he used to fund a new R&D facility in Shenstone.[1] What did it do? The facility continued work on the Wankel rotary engine, which, if successful, would power a new Norton motorcycle. Ultimately, several hundred nearly hand-built, rotary-engined Nortons were produced, typically with scavenged chassis and components.

Poore died in 1987, and ownership of the marque remained contentious for many years. To date, no commercially viable Norton has been produced.

Bert Hopwood died at his country retreat in Torquay in 1996. His lasting legacy may have been his autobiography, *Whatever Happened to the British Motorcycle Industry?* Originally published in 1981, it's an insider's look at the industry but also unmistakably an apologia for his failures.

The Meriden co-op did not succeed, although it lasted from 1975 until 1983. Geoffrey Robinson resigned from his position at Jaguar in 1975 and was elected to Parliament in 1976; he also served as the chief executive and later unpaid advisor to the co-op for several years. Tony Benn did not succeed in nationalizing British industry, and he gave up his seat in the House of Commons in 2001, stating that he did so "to devote more time to politics."[2]

Initially, all workers at the Meriden co-op were cross-trained and paid 50 pounds a week, except for the chief financial officer, who was recruited from outside the plant. Several studies say productivity increased by half or more, however, meeting one of the aims of its socialist backers. In time, though, plenty of exceptions to the flat wage scale crept in as the co-op needed to recruit workers with requisite skills.[3]

Plenty of postmortems were conducted. Among the causes of death offered were that the workers were unable to service the government loan they received at start-up; the English currency had been revalued, making the bikes more expensive in export markets; and no truly new models were ever offered, though the co-op eventually added electric starting and eight-valve cylinder heads. But Edward Turner would have understood at least one reason for the Meriden bike's failure — the bikes didn't look right, being burdened with a motley batch of styling cues ranging from the original Speed Twin of 1937 to more angular 1970s influences to that electric starter of late that stuck out of the engine like a goiter.

Although it is the thesis of this book that the British motorcycle industry has ended, a new Triumph motorcycle factory opened in Hinckley, Leicestershire, in 1991. John Bloor, a former plasterer who made his millions in real estate, bought the Triumph name after the workers' co-operative folded in 1983; he outbid Enfield (India) for the rights. Bloor licensed Les Harris, a parts supplier in Devon, to assemble a few more Bonnevilles over the next several years, while he assembled a small team of engineers and designers. The first of the Hinckley Triumphs were thoroughly modern, liquid-cooled, multi-cylinder machines with some modular characteristics (the three- and four-cylinder models shared many parts). They bore no resemblance to the old, air-cooled, vertical twins the brand had been famous for, and Bloor said that was the message he meant to send — this was the *new* Triumph. Yet by the turn of the century, Triumph began making a series of retro-styled, air-cooled twins, even down to the wire-spoke wheels, which have proved very popular again. The company is successful and sold 37,600 machines overall in fiscal year 2006, with double-digit growth expected for the next several years. Japan is a major export market.

Notes

Introduction

i Boston Consulting Group, *Strategy Alternatives for the British Motorcycle Industry: A Report Prepared for the Secretary of State for Industry* (London: Her Majesty's Stationery Office, 1975), 5.

ii Don Morley, *BSA* (London: Osprey Publishing, 1991), 25.

iii Cited in Chris Hemming, "The Meriden Motorcycle Co-Operative: An Unconventional End to the Decline of a British Industry?" www.labour-history.org.uk/support_files/Meriden1.pdf

Chapter One: Patriarchs

1 Mark Forster, "The Mayor Who Was Forced to Stand Down: We Look at Coventry Mayor Siegfried Bettmann Shunned Because of His German Links," *Coventry Evening Telegraph*, 1 April 2000: 6–7.

2 Jeff Clew, *Turner's Triumphs: Edward Turner and His Triumph Motorcycles* (Dorchester: Veloce Publishing, 2000), 16.

3 Edward Turner, audiotaped interview with Jim Lee, 1971, courtesy of Jeremy Mortimore, an Ariel bicycle historian.

4 Bert Hopwood, *Whatever Happened to the British Motorcycle Industry?* (Sparkford, Yeovil, Somerset: Haynes Publishing, 1998), 9.

5 Clew, *Turner's Triumphs*, 11–15; Barbara M.D. Smith, "Turner, Edward (1901–1973), Motorcycle Designer and Manufacturer," *Oxford Dictionary of National Biography* (Oxford: Oxford University Press, 2004), http://www.oxforddnb.com/index/101048349 (subscription required); http://en.wikipedia.org/wiki/Edward_Turner

6 Turner, interview with Lee.

7 Hopwood, *Whatever Happened*, 25.

8 Frank Griffiths, "Driving Force," *Classic Bike*, July 1993: 16–17.

9 "The Motorcycle Hall of Fame Museum: Bill Johnson" (inducted 2005),

http://www.motorcyclemuseum.org/halloffame/hofbiopage.asp?id=372

10 Sean Hawker, "The Unsung Heroes," *Classic Bike*, June 1994: 16–19.

11 Carl Chinn, "Remember When: The Night the Whole City Seemed Ablaze," *Birmingham Evening Mail*, 19 November 2005: 28.

12 Donovan M. Ward, *The Other Battle: Being a History of the Birmingham Small Arms Co. Ltd.* . . . (York: Ben Johnson, 1946), 47.

13 Don Morley, BSA (London: Osprey Automotive, 1991), 17.

14 Owen Wright, BSA: *The Complete Story* (Marlborough: Crowood Press, 1992), 39.

15 Clew, *Turner's Triumphs*, 37–38.

16 Hopwood, *Whatever Happened*, 39.

17 Turner, interview with Lee.

18 Hopwood, *Whatever Happened*, 47.

19 Hopwood, *Whatever Happened*, 63.

20 "Turner's Twin," *Classic Bike*, March 1978: 45.

Chapter Two: Racer's Edge

1 Geoff Duke, *Geoff Duke: In Pursuit of Perfection* (London: Osprey Publishing, 1988), 9–13.

2 "Most Dangerous Race Claims over 170 Lives," *Belfast News Letter*, 30 May 2003: 7.

3 Mick Woolett, *Norton: The Complete Illustrated History* (St. Paul, MN: Motorbooks, 2004), 21.

4 "F.L. Beart, Tuner and Enthusiast," *The Motor Cycle*, 25 August 1938: 281.

5 Woolett, *Norton*, 219.

6 Roy Bacon, BSA *Gold Star and Other Singles* (London: Osprey, 1982), 26–29.

7 Woolett, *Norton*, 199.

8 Duke, *Geoff Duke*, 19.

9 David Booth, "Terrifying TT on the Isle of Man: Steep, Sharp, and Rough Roads Barely Describe the World's Toughest Motorcycle Course," *Edmonton Journal*, 6 July 2004: T2.

10 Roland Pike, unpublished memoirs, "Chapter 17: How the MC1 Racer Brought Me to the Factory," www.restorenik.com/daytona/RP_chp_17.htm

11 The company is still in business but sells Harley-Davidson today.

12 Jerry Hatfield, "David and Goliath," *The Classic MotorCycle*, May 1992: 4–8.

13 "Motorcycle Hall of Fame, Pickerington, OH: Dick Klamfoth," http://www.motorcyclemuseum.org/halloffame/hofbiopage.asp?id=71

14 Lisa A. Miller, "Full Throttle into Racing History," *Lake George [NY] Mirror*, 1 June 2001: 21.

15 Bert Hopwood, *Whatever Happened to the British Motorcycle Industry?* (Sparkford, Yeovil, Somerset: Haynes Publishing, 1998), 109.

16 Some reports say Pike headed the race team at Daytona in 1954, but Dick Klamfoth, who rode one of the BSA machines at Daytona in 1954, and Pike's unpublished memoirs both assert that he was not there that year.

17 Roland Pike, unpublished memoirs, "Chapter 28: My Trips to the USA," www.restorenik.com/daytona/RP_chp_28.htm

18 Peter Glover, "Tribute to Industry Giant Bert Hopwood," *The Classic MotorCycle*, January 1997:57.

19 Woolett, *Norton*, 94–95.

Chapter Three: The Continental Circus

1 Peter Glover, "Factory Finish," *The Classic MotorCycle*, August 1993: 30–33.

2 Norman Vanhouse, former works rider and manager at BSA, personal communication, 4 July 2006. Additional details from *The Best of Everything*, a BSA industrial film about life at the factory produced circa 1960.

3 Norman Vanhouse, BSA *Competition History* (Sparkford, Yeovil, Somerset: Haynes Publishing, 1986), 71.

4 Paul Stephens, *Moto-Cross: The Golden Years* (London: Osprey Automotive, 1998), 149.

5 Speedway racers typically employ 500 cc motors in ultra-lightweight frames with little or no suspension or brakes; the bikes compete on flat, oval, dirt tracks in closed courses and slide through the turns.

6 Brian Martin, "Martin on Nicholson," *The Classic MotorCycle*, January 1994: 13.

7 Ed Youngblood, "The History of Motocross, Part Two: Motocross Goes International 1947 through 1965," www.motorcyclemuseum.org/exhibits/MX/history/part2.asp

8 Bill Nicholson, "My Biggest Mistake," *The Classic MotorCycle*, June 1992: 69.

Chapter Four: Mods and Rockers

1 Owen Wright, BSA: *The Complete Story* (Marlborough: Crowood Press, 1992), 45.

2 Laurie Padgham, letter to the editor, *Derby Evening Telegraph*, 10 April 2006: 4.

3 Barry Ryerson, *The Giants of Small Heath: The History of BSA* (Henley-on-Thames: G.T. Foulis, 1980), 149–50.

4 Ibid., 150.

5 R.P.T. Davenport-Hines, *Dudley Docker: The Life and Times of a Trade Warrior* (Cambridge, UK: Press Syndicate of the University of Cambridge, 1984), 231–32.

6 Bob Holliday, *The Story of BSA Motorcycles* (Cambridge, UK: Patrick Stephens, 1978), 100.

7   Ryerson, *The Giants of Small Heath*, 111.

8   See http://www.statistics.gov.uk/StatBase/xsdataset.asp?more=Y&vlnk=1464&All=Y&B2.x

9   Barbara M.D. Smith, "The History of the British Motorcycle Industry 1945–1975," Centre for Urban and Regional Studies, University of Birmingham Occasional Papers, 1981, Table 2 and Table 3, 11 and 12.

10 "If You're Not the No. 1 in the World, You Can't Be No. 1 in Japan," http://world.honda.com/history

11 Karel Williams, John Williams, and Dennis Thomas, *Why Are the British Bad at Manufacturing?* (Henley-on-Thames: Routledge and Kegan Paul, 1983), 28.

12 Boston Consulting Group, *Strategy Alternatives for the British Motorcycle Industry: A Report Prepared for the Secretary of State for Industry* (London: Her Majesty's Stationery Office, 1975), 50.

13 Joe Heaton, "An Examination of the Post-Second World War Relative Decline of UK Manufacturing 1945–1975, Viewed through the Lens of the Birmingham Small Arms Company Ltd." (PhD diss., University of Birmingham, 2007), 142.

14 Donald J. Brown, phone conversation with the author, 2006.

15 Hughie Hancox, *Tales of Triumph Motorcycles and the Meriden Factory* (Dorchester: Veloce Publishing, 1996), 39.

16 Ryerson, *The Giants of Small Heath*, 151–54.

17 Roland Pike, unpublished memoirs, "Chapter 18: The Development Shop and Clubmans TT," www.restorenik.com/daytona/RP_chp_18.htm

18 Mick Duckworth, "Percy Tait: Making the Bonneville Better," *Classic Bike*, September 2003: 57.

19 Hancox, *Tales of Triumph Motorcycles*, 84–86.

20 Duckworth, "Percy Tait," 58.

21 Harry Sucher, "Harley-Davidson's Oriental Interlude," *Antique Motorcycle*, Winter 2005: 18–22.

22 Dorothy Child-Jones, "Harley-Davidson Pioneer Alfred Rich Child: A Man of Firsts," *A Century of Motorcycles, Easyriders Style*, contained in the vertical file, Motorcycle Hall of Fame Museum, Pickerington, OH, 34.

23 Alfred Rich Child, "A.R. Child's Recollections of Harley-Davidson Motorcycle Sales in Japan from 1922 to the Present Day," typescript, 1977, on file at the Motorcycle Hall of Fame and Museum, Pickerington, OH.

24 Some details in this section come from Martin Jack Rosenblum, "Harley-Davidson in Japan: The Early Years," undated internal document copyright Harley-Davidson Motor Company. Other details are from Child's 1977 typescript.

25 Bert Hopwood, *Whatever Happened to the British Motorcycle Industry?* (Sparkford, Yeovil, Somerset: Haynes Publishing, 1998), 110–11.

26 Ibid., 151.

27 Alan Cathcart, "The Mighty Apollo," *Australian Motorcycle News*, 11 April 2003: 34–43.

28 Mick Duckworth, "Just Ace," *Classic Bike*, September 1994: 30.

29 Alan Seeley, "Rockers," *Classic Bike*, May 2007: 61.

30 Mike Nicks, "Turner's Twin," *Classic Bike*, March 1978: 45.

Chapter Five: The Last World Champion

1   Much information for this section comes from http://world. honda.com/history; Robert L. Shook, *Honda: An American Success Story* (Upper Saddle River, NJ: Prentice-Hall, 1988); and Graham Sanderson, "Honda's Half-Century," *Classic Bike*, July 1998: 50–66.

2   Harvard Business School, *Note on the Motorcycle Industry — 1975* (Cambridge, MA: Harvard Business School Publishing, 1978), 2.

3   Geoff Duke, *Geoff Duke: In Pursuit of Perfection* (London: Osprey Publishing, 1988), 170–76.

4   Ivor Davies, *It's a Triumph* (Henley-on-Thames: G.T. Foulis, 1980), 200–05.

5   Sanderson, "Honda's Half-Century," 59.

6   Barbara M.D. Smith, "The History of the British Motorcycle Industry 1945–1975," Centre for Urban and Regional Studies, University of Birmingham Occasional Papers, 1981, 5.

7   Boston Consulting Group, *Strategy Alternatives for the British Motorcycle Industry: A Report Prepared for the Secretary of State for Industry* (London: Her Majesty's Stationery Office, 1975), 37.

8   Richard T. Pascale, "Perspectives on Strategy: The Real Story behind Honda's Success," *California Management Review* 26.3 (1984): 47–72.

9   Owen Wright, *BSA: The Complete Story* (Marlborough: Crowood Press, 1992), 44.

10 Barry Ryerson, *The Giants of Small Heath: The History of BSA* (Henley-on-Thames: G.T. Foulis, 1980), 159.

11 Bert Hopwood, *Whatever Happened to the British Motorcycle Industry?* (Sparkford, Yeovil, Somerset: Haynes, 1998), 201–02.

12 Frank Melling, "Tunes of Glory," *Classic Bike*, January 2002: 24.

13 Mick Woolett, *Norton: The Complete Illustrated History* (St. Paul, MN: Motorbooks, 2004), 276.

14 Ibid., 279, 282.

15 Mick Walker, *Mike Hailwood: The Fans' Favourite* (Derby, UK: Breedon Books, 2005), 100.

16 Ibid., 98.

Chapter Six: Industrial Action

1   Mick Duckworth, "The Mighty Twin," *Classic Bike*, December 2006: 68.

2   The source for the sales estimate is Mike Jackson, former European sales manager for Norton Villiers Triumph, the successor to Norton Villiers.

3   Peter Glover, "Tribute to Industry Giant, Bert Hopwood," *Classic Bike*, January 1997, 57.

4   The quotation refers to the British predilection for projecting sales, then adjusting production to that estimate. A good year was when they sold out all production.

5   Bert Hopwood, *Whatever Happened to the British Motorcycle Industry* (Sparkford, Yeovil, Somerset: Haynes Publishing, 1998), 207.

6   Frank Melling, "A Thoughtful Genius . . . ," *Daily Telegraph* [London], 1 December 2001: 13.

7   Frank Melling, "Tunes of Glory," *Classic Bike*, January 2002: 27.

8   "2004 Honda CBR1000RR In-Line Four History," Honda press release, www.sportrider.com/bikes/2004/146_04_honda_cbr_engine_history.

9   Bob Holliday, *The Story of BSA Motor Cycles* (Cambridge, UK: Patrick Stephens, 1978), 118.

10   Joe Heaton, "An Examination of the Post-Second World War Relative Decline of UK Manufacturing 1945–1975, Viewed through the Lens of the Birmingham Small Arms Company Ltd." (PhD diss., University of Birmingham, 2007), 136–37.

11   Bob Holliday, *The Story of BSA*, 118.

12   Owen Wright, *BSA: The Complete Story* (Marlborough: Crowood Press, 1992), 159–61.

13   Mick Duckworth, "What if . . . ," *Classic Bike*, February 2007: 56–60.

14   Boston Consulting Group, *Strategy Alternatives for the British Motorcycle Industry: A Report Prepared for the Secretary of State for Industry* (London: Her Majesty's Stationery Office, 1975), 35.

15   Barry Ryerson, *The Giants of Small Heath* (Henley-on-Thames: G.T. Foulis, 1980), 174–75.

16   "BSA Certain of Significant First Half Loss, Lord Shawcross Says," *Times* [London], 6 December 1972: 21.

17   Ryerson, *The Giants of Small Heath*, 179.

18   Don Brown and Craig Vetter, "The Hurricane Dialogue: The True Story of the Triumph Hurricane as Told by the Men Who Made It Happen," interview conducted by Ed Youngblood, transcript dated July 2004, www.motohistory.net/featuredstory/vetter-story1.html and at Vetter's website, www.craigvetter.com.

19   *Meriden: Historical Summary, 1972–1974* (London: Burrup, Mathieson, 1974), 1.

20   Ryerson, *The Giants of Small Heath*, 181.

21   Heaton, "Examination," 174.

22   Anthony Rowley, "Big Profits Setback for both BSA and Norton Shown in Merger Offer," *Times* [London], 8 June 1973: 23.

23   Clifford Webb, "One-Sixth at Triumph . . . ," *Times* [London], 21 July 1973: 21.

24   *Meriden: Historical Summary*, 7–8.

25   John R. Nelson, e-mail to the author, 28 July 2008. Mr. Nelson generally eschews interviews on the subject and refers interested parties to the *Coventry Evening Telegraph* newspaper files for what he terms unbiased reporting on both the sit-in and the co-op.

26 Peter Morgan, "Rather You than Me," *Socialist Review* 269 (2002), http://pubs.socialistreviewindex.org.uk/sr269/morgan.htm

27 Tony Benn, *Against the Tide: Diaries 1973–76*, ed. Ruth Winstone (London: Hutchinson, 1989), 118, cited in Chris Hemming, "The Meriden Motorcycle Co-Operative: An Experiment in Workers' Democracy or a Bizarre End to the British Motorcycle Industry?" www.labour-history.org.uk/support_files/Meriden2.pdf

28 M.E. Fairclough, "The Political Economy of Producer Co-Operatives: A Study of Triumph Motorcycle (Meriden) Ltd. and Britain's Industrial Decline" (PhD diss., Bristol University, 37-6953), 319, cited in Hemming, "The Meriden Motorcycle Co-Operative."

29 Letter from Geoffrey Robinson to Tony Benn, 24 June 1974, cited in Hemming, "The Meriden Motorcycle Co-Operative."

30 "British Cabinet Papers 1975 — Wilson Was Faced with Revolt over Benn Move," *Irish News*, 29 December 2005: 29.

31 William Colquhoun, former managing direct of NVT International, Ltd., disputes the quote. He says Poore actually said, "Show me an asset and I'll strip it." Private communication with Colquhoun, November 2008.

32 Edward Townsend, "Small Heath Men Heckle Mr. Benn . . . ," *Times* [London], 9 November 1974: 21.

33 Clifford Webb, "Unions Urge Complete Takeover of NVT," *Times* [London], 20 November 1974: 21.

34 Dennis Poore, "Reasons for NVT's 7.4 Million Pound Loss," *Times* [London], 29 July 1975: 16.

35 Frank Melling, "Norton that Lost Its Pull," *Daily Telegraph* [London], 27 January 2007: 10.

Epilogue

1 "NVT Happy with 2.3 Million [Pounds] Meriden Settlement," *Times* [London], 5 May 1977: 26.

2 Dale Williams, "Dudley: Legendary Labour Stalwart Is Special Guest at Celebration of Chainmaker's Protest," *Birmingham Evening Mail* [Staffordshire edition], 12 September 2007: 24.

3 Clifford Webb, "Will the Meriden Deal Finally Triumph?" *Times* [London], 9 February 1977: 19.

Index

decries British motorcycle industry in letter to *The Times*, 123–24; dies, 136

Turner, Eric, 92, 120

Tushingham, Rita (appeared in *The Leather Boys*), 74

Two-factory model, 124

Umberslade Hall (officially known as Group Engineering Centre), xiv, 85, 112–14

Vanhouse, Norman (competes successfully in 1952 ISDT), 47; visits abandoned BSA factory in Small Heath, 132

Velocette motorcycles (Thruxton model), xii; history, 3; wins Isle of Man Junior TT in 1949, 28; Viceroy scooter, 74

Vetter, Craig (American motorcycle stylist), 121

Villiers (produced small two-stroke motors), 97

Vincent motorcycles, 42; sets land speed record in 1948, 71–72

Vorster, Emil, 77

Wankel motorcycle engine, 113, 136

Webster, Ernie, 116

Weistrich, David (American bicycle parts importer), 67

Wickes, Jack (Edward Turner's "pencil"), 14

Wilson, Harold (British prime minister), 127

Wolverhampton (Norton Villiers production), 105, 124, 130, 132

Youngblood, Ed (motorcycle historian), 53